Coming into Balance

A Guide for Activating Your True Potential

Coming into Balance

A Guide for Activating Your True Potential

Jane Ely D.MIN.

parvati
press

Parvati Press books may be purchased for educational, business, or sales promotional use.

Printed on acid-free paper

Book layout and design by Susan Caldwell, Susan Caldwell Design,
susan@scaldwelldesign.com
Cover photograph by George Steinmetz/Corbis Images

Published by Parvati Press, New York, NY
www.parvatipress.com

Visit the author website:
www.drjaneely.net

Library of Congress Control Number: 2014959977

ISBN:
(ebook) 978-1-942523-01-7
(paperback) 978-1-942523-00-0

The star ancestors, the earth keepers, and the teachers
who walked this path before us
and kept the visions alive in our bones
so that we remember their wisdom,
passed through oral tradition generation to generation
showing us how to live in balance
in the Peaceful Blessing Way.

We dedicate healing ourselves,
coming back into balance with mother earth
so that we leave a better foundation
upon which you can stand strong and in beauty
in the conscious journey
of the Peaceful Blessing Way.

foreword

Creator,
We call forth
the global awakening of humanity
in peace filled consciousness,
NOW!

When this book began to find its way through me five years ago, I thought it would be a simple task to follow the direction that Spirit asked of me – to describe and share the Medicine Wheel as a universal guide for transformation with step by step practical activations that I have been practicing and teaching for many years. Ha! That was a Spirit joke and a sneak-up dance to get me motivated. My intention was and still is to bring the ancient indigenous knowledge from the past into present. The Medicine Wheel is a mandala found in Native American Indian, First Nations, Tibetan, Hindu, African, Aboriginal Australian, Celtic, Mayan, Aztec, Incan cultures to name only a few. The Circle of Life or Medicine Wheel is part of our collective intelligence. It can be found on ancient cave walls all over the world, in petroglyphs, earth works, stone circles, temples, engraved stone calendars, sand paintings, etc. I have been working with the Medicine Wheel most of my life as a means of awakening.

I have always been a listener. I have listened to Spirit from my earliest memories. I have a running dialogue with the Creator that has taken me all over the world, put me in the path of many teachers and guided me unfailingly in the medicine way of faith, trust, truth, and discernment – the Four Cardinal Directions of the great Wheel of Life. I have also always been able to interpret and somehow describe that which Spirit is showing me as a means of teaching others and bringing consciousness forth into this world. In this way I have grown into a Life Task that I consciously remember agreeing to in The Before Time or more commonly known as Life Between Lives. One of my jobs this lifetime is as a networker, an ambassador, and a conductor linking bridges and wisdom between many traditions and worlds.

As I accessed the information inculcated in my DNA in writing the book, I began to envision it more and more as a workbook to bring healing, reflection and insights through self-discovery and spiritual practices. When I began the book I realized the world is on a dangerous trajectory course towards self-destruction. Everyone my age range born in the 1950s onward has been experiencing humanity's inhumanity towards self, Mother Earth and all her relations. The volume of self-destruction is now reaching crescendos never before witnessed. The Inquisition, The Holocaust, and other notable evils we have enacted here upon Planet Earth have been the warm-up act to darkness that is being perpetrated all over the globe. My description of evil "is the conscious intention to do harm to self or others."

Barbara Hand Clow in her book entitled *The Pleiadian Agenda* foreshadows our present state of global chaos from the point of view that we are being manipulated by "the World Management Team" – who definitely do not have humanity's collective good on their agenda.

The point is that the time of sitting on the sidelines waiting for things to change or be magically corrected is over. This book began to take on a deeper meaning as a tool belt full of practical, readily accessible knowledge and skills to change humanity's consciousness on a global level. We have medicines, antidotes and homeopathic responses to re-align with our birthright here on Mother Earth. Our birthright is to live peacefully with hope, and in right relationship with all other living beings. As the teachings deepened for me while writing the book, I understood more about Spirit directing me to birth *Coming into Balance: A Guide for Activating Your True Potential* as a field guide to practice and share daily. Coming into balance is an intention and a call for action. We all need to align constantly and consistently with our soul's gifts. We are here to activate them in order to create individual and global transformation. Giving energy to what is wrong feeds the monster that is energetically running amuck in our minds and on the planet. Giving conscious energy to all Earth Beings' birthright of peace, balance, inclusivity, and community provides a new energy that feeds a collective consciousness growing all over Mother Earth. Nothing new there, you may well say. Noble aspirations and there are so many great teachers and books out there all bringing the same message.

What is new is the perspective from which it is written and the step-by-step guide that comes with a guarantee. As the book took form, I realized that there were about 20+ years of spiritual practices I have either been taught by elders or Spirit has taught me through my life experiences coalescing in the manuscript and graphics. This guide to activating your true potential is a synthesis of knowledge, practical practices and it's also fun.

Here's the catch and a guarantee. As the book evolved I felt compelled to bring spiritual practice into daily life as a means to dissolve resistance, ignorance and complacency. Spirituality means rolling up your sleeves, picking up a shovel and digging deep. It means doing what is right. Part of spiritual practice is meeting your shadow self. The section on *The Masks* in this book is an essential spiritual everyday practice, living life with courage and commitment. This book is not for the lazy or the weak of heart. It is not for the *new ager* who would rather skip over the shadow work that is difficult in favor of hanging around up in the rafters of life. Part of our overall malaise as a species relates to our refusal to deal with our shadow side. Acknowledging and feeling discomfort, grief, and sadness is essential for our healing. As is creating a safe vessel in which to heal these aspects of our humanity. Practical means create a grounded vessel for evolution.

We can commit to work with these aspects of self and our world as *medicines* rather than negative energies that get projected outwardly onto self, others and ultimately onto Mother Earth. The exercises and information in this book speak directly to going on an archaeological dig. Here is the promise. If you follow the book as it is written, do the exercises and walk the Medicine Wheel in all its levels and layers as described, you will be a changed and a more awake and aware being at the end of the book. Not a bad guarantee, eh?

Here's the challenge. Once you get through this book, start it again but with a group whom you think would be interested in going on this journey of conscious awakening with you. Book clubs, meditation groups, family circles, school children, tai chi groups, senior citizens gatherings, or with your beloved partner, etc. We can all work together in community to teach one another and share wisdom, insight and transformative experiences as we walk the Medicine Wheel. No one person is the leader – we all are because we are in the circle of life. I request these groups be free, that nobody charges a fee for anyone to attend and that the community is open to anyone who can commit to going through the workbook/journal from beginning to completion.

My vision for this book is for it to travel around the world to get circles of consciousness set-up – to start Medicine Wheel working groups; to plant the seeds, give you driving instructions and then witness you as you take off with the wisdom teachings as you bring your experiences, knowledge and insights into the world. I see concentric circles of awakened aware beings as a matrix of healing expands globally. The teachings are universal, meaning they are matrix oriented – like the webbing of all life growing in balance globally, consciously.

Eckhart Tolle, in his book *A New Earth* makes this call for self-responsible action. "Are you polluting the world or cleaning up the mess? You are responsible for your inner space, nobody else is, just as you are responsible for the planet. As within, so without. If humans clear inner pollution, then they will cease to create outer pollution."

DRIVING INSTRUCTIONS

Start at the beginning. Follow the teachings as they are outlined step by step. Do not skip over any skillful means exercise, no matter how simple it may seem to you. Transformation is an inside job. It takes time, space, patience and commitment. Spiritual arrogance is lethal. Pace yourself and give each practice the space and reflection it deserves. Keep a journal as you walk the Medicine Wheel. Watch your dreams as well. They will inform you on many levels. Use your creativity as you walk the wheel to describe in poem or stream of consciousness writing, painting, or collage the insights and awakenings. Above all, use this book to heal the past so that you can live fully in the present moment. The Mask work is essential to healing the past as is The Witness, Inquirer, Experiencer work and meditations. After all, the present moment is all there truly is. So let's live consciously NOW!

Breathe deeply while reading and doing the exercises. Laugh out loud – a lot. Laughter shakes up the mind-field.

I'll see you at the Center of the Medicine Wheel – the place of Balance.

BLESSINGS AND LOVE, *Jane*

Are you polluting the world
or cleaning up the mess?
You are responsible for your inner space,
nobody else is, just as you are responsible for the planet.
As within, so without.
If humans clear inner pollution,
then they will cease to create outer pollution.

ECKHART TOLLE, IN HIS BOOK *A NEW EARTH*
MAKES THIS CALL FOR SELF-RESPONSIBLE ACTION.

contents

1

a guide for activating your true potential

We who have lost our sense and our senses –
our touch, our smell, our vision of who we are;
We who frantically force and press all things,
without rest for body or spirit,
hurting our earth and injuring ourselves:
we call a halt.
We want to rest.
We need to rest and allow the earth to rest.
We need to reflect and to rediscover the mystery that lives in us,
that is the ground of every unique expression of life,
the source of the fascination that calls all things to communion.
We declare a Sabbath, a space of quiet:
for simply being and letting be;
for recovering the great forgotten truths,
for learning how to live again.

PRAYER FROM THE U. N. ENVIRONMENTAL SABBATH PROGRAM (EARTH PRAYERS)

INTRODUCTION

This is a book about coming back into balance through the use of skillful means – the proverbial tool belt of practices and insights for creative, personal and global transformation. It is also about finding sensate experiences within our body, mind, heart and spirit, learning to activate and develop them and fine tune them as tools for conscious awareness and change. The ancient wheel of spiritual evolution has basic principles: Trust, Truth, Discernment and Faith, each represents a direction in the Medicine Wheel, as well as, an element of earth, water, air and fire. The fifth element is Space, THE-GREAT-MYSTERY-THAT-MOVES-THROUGH-ALL-THINGS. These are represented in the Above, Below and Center Directions of the Medicine Wheel. We will learn how to reconnect with these and activate them in our daily lives.

I look at this work as a "field guide for life", a manual for self-awareness, discovery and self-recovery as we navigate these very uncertain times. Each of the practices in the book arises from my spiritual growth and the teachings I have been fortunate to receive from many wise elders who are named throughout the text. Also, each of the practices comes from a deep well of knowledge I have developed and practiced in reclaiming and healing my life. My intention is to share the teachings in a grounded, unique way that is practical and also provides a *jump start* for anyone needing to heal their life. We will work with how to wake up from *trance-states*, the meaning of trances and the meaning of Masks, also known as defense mechanisms, that keep us stuck in the past. How to get free of *story* and go beyond into a state of awakened freedom.

It is time to get through the past, collect the nuggets of insight and wisdom and get on with living large as manifesting change-makers. It is also time to take responsibility for the past but not dwell in it. We will explore the eco-psychology of our personal environment as it relates to the outer physical and inner spiritual worlds through the twelve teachings of the Wheel of Life.

|NOTE| *I use the terms Medicine Wheel and Wheel of Life, Circle of Life interchangeably. This relates to a collective understanding rather than to one culture.*

Each section has exercises and self-reflective techniques that I call *skillful means* for deep lasting personal change. I practice these *skillful means* and I know they work, as do my students and clients to whom I teach Energy Medicine and Eco-psychology.

Albert Einstein has often been quoted as saying, "There are only two ways to live your life. One is as though nothing is a miracle. The other is as though everything is a miracle." I feel it is crucial to activate and manifest change on a global level by embracing this wisdom. It starts with you and me.

It is time to find the visionary prophetic healer within, to dream creative dreams, to bring back the sacred in every day life. As Hawaiian kumu (teacher), Maka'ala Yates says, "It is time to start a positive epidemic". This positive epidemic is a tsunami of transformational healing. It is happening now. We are on this wave together.

2

THE MEDICINE WHEEL OF LIFE
what the wheel of life teaches us

Everything is holy;
Holy is thy name,
Forests, mountains, oceans.
Listen to the sound.
Great Spirit's wisdom
lives within us.

UNKNOWN AUTHOR
NATIVE AMERICAN INDIAN SONG

The Twelve Teachings
1. wholeness
2. change
3. cycles
4. realities
5. learning | growth
6. four directions
   and dimensions
7. development
8. participation |
   engagement
9. patience | will
10. commitment
11. remembering
12. the sacred wheel
    of life

WHAT THE WHEEL OF LIFE TEACHES US

The Medicine Wheel is a sacred circle teaching us about human development, our inter-relatedness with all life, insights, conscious awakening, skillful means, rites of passage, important things to remember, ways to create inner balance and how to be in harmony with all sentient life. The teachings are given in non-linear, circular fashion, meaning that the wheel is constantly turning – bringing new insights and awarenesses forward in support of the different phases of life we live.

The Medicine Wheel teachings are universal, residing in our collective DNA awaiting awakening. There are twelve teachings that support human evolution on the spiritual, physical, emotional and mental levels. Each aspect of the teachings activates a *sense* that is part of our true nature. Re-awakening these senses is our birthright and our task in order to live our true potential. By reconnecting and practicing *skillful means* in consciously aware states, we are transforming our life, and growing our soul. We are also taking responsibility for our lives, the health of Mother Earth, creating new pathways of healing and reconciliation for the future generations who will come after us.

the twelve teachings

the medicine wheel

north

air
white
discernment
clarity
mental world

above

father sky & sun
mother moon
star nations

west

water
black
truth
introspection
emotional world

center : *now direction*

east

fire
yellow
faith
illumination
spiritual world

below

devic kingdom
mother earth intelligence

south

earth
red
trust
innocence
physical world

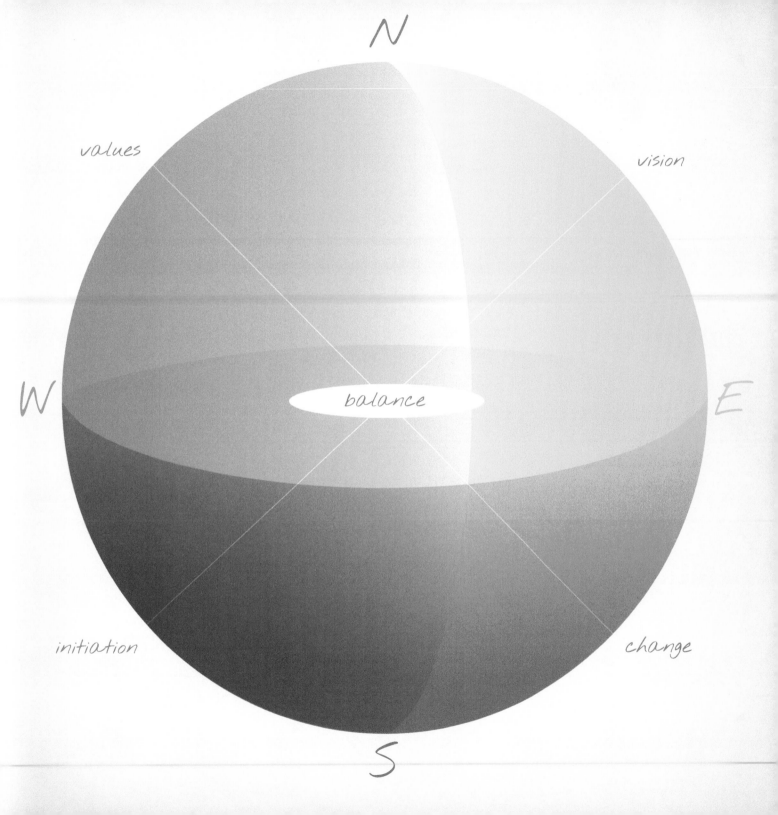

A universal truth is everything is sacred, that all things have life and that all life is interrelated. The universe is whole; we are part of it as well as being reflections of it.

We are holographic by nature in that within each of us is a universe of knowledge, a divine spark of soul that reflects and is part of the universal soul. *Uni* in Latin means one. We are all capable of unity consciousness. Through self-exploration and self-awareness we maintain a relationship with all life in a balanced and harmonious way.

We are not separate from anything. We are part of every thing. We are whole. We must remind ourselves of this by practicing it daily. Fold your daily life into your spiritual understanding and practice.

We have forgotten that we are in relationship with all life. We are larger than an individual living a life of survival which separates us from all other life experiences. We are connected to a greater whole.

SKILLFUL MEANS

Take a moment to check inside yourself. Feel your interior self. Do you feel a sense of wholeness living within you, or do you feel fragmented? Note those times when you recognize that you feel whole, connected to some greater force larger than yourself.

When does this happen? Perhaps when you are looking at the night sky full of stars, or when you are out for a walk and notice birds flying by, or when you see a baby smile for the first time, or when you look at jewel toned leaves on trees in the changing of seasons. Wholeness is an inner sense, a knowing and an understanding. It comes from connecting your inner nature with outer nature. It arises from within as you consciously make an effort to seek out

Skillful Means Journal

Skillful Means Journal

the sense of wholeness. Wholeness is a living, breathing aspect of being human. It is an awareness that feels round and full inside. Wholeness is a deep truth that cannot be denied, nor broken, nor torn asunder. It feels like equanimity. It is quiet, sure and steady. Wholeness is a sacred moment when recognized and integrated consciously as being here now – as being sacred.

Cultivate wholeness and experience it growing.

You may also experience wholeness from the perspective of "what it is not". Oftentimes, we get to a sensibility by describing our way around it, defining what it isn't and then homing in on what it is. This may be useful in awakening you to how much of your being does not experience wholeness. Do not dwell upon the "lack of experiencing wholeness". Find a moment, in which you feel the spark, or glimmer of wholeness. Seek out ways to recognize it when it happens and grow this aspect of your sensing wholeness each day. Make it fun, an insight practice like the *skillful means* described below.

SKILLFUL MEANS

Take a moment to define what wholeness is inside of you. Journal it, or draw it. Find a creative way to describe wholeness for yourself. Sit with this sense for five minutes. Keep returning to it every time another thought pops up in your mind. Breathe, returning to being whole. Breathe, experiencing yourself as whole. Breathe, experiencing life as whole. Breathe, experiencing your life as whole. Breathe, experiencing the world as whole. Every time you drop the sense of being whole, simply return to wholeness. Keep breathing and smile with inner wholeness. When you practice this during your day, begin to notice changes in how you are experiencing life.

Creation is in constant motion. Nothing is static. Chaos is part of creation. Order is also part of creation. These energies of creation-chaos and creation-order are both necessary for life. There are three truths about change. They are as follows:

When we are in a creation-change-wave (which is all the time), we experience the energy of development, the coming together of things, or an *aha* moment of insight. This can also be experienced as a sense of movement or a building type of energy. But this phase is not static. It moves continually. The next place the energy will go is known as stasis. This is experienced as stillness, a pause, a breath, a moment of quiet. Stasis is very mysterious. It is space and nothingness. Stasis is full of the unknown – the proverbial pregnant pause. After stasis arises the third part of the change wave, dissolution or disintegration. It is the coming apart or the letting go of something. Change is constant and it is something upon which we can depend.

Change is organic. It brings us to one of the greatest teachings of our life – that everything and everyone is impermanent. Nothing lasts forever in the material outer world. If we continually try to control change, we miss living life.

Change moves continually in a wave-like energy. Look to nature to see how change is happening all the time. Go to a lake, river, or the ocean to observe how endlessly the waves move upon the waters. This mysterious energy also lives inside of each sentient being upon the planet. It is inside of you at this very moment, arising with each breath you take. The waves are moving upon the shores of your being. How we consciously ride the waves of change makes all the difference between living an open life with flexibility and flow versus experiencing change with resistance, rigidity and dread. The first choice is to live with an openhearted energy that embraces change, looking forward to life with enthusiasm, being engaged and participating fully with the changes arising. The other way of being with change is to take it as a hardship, a challenge to be surmounted, something to struggle through, yet one more task to heap upon an already overwhelming life. This is draining energetically and it will affect the physical, mental, emotional and spiritual bodies.

SKILLFUL MEANS

Eckhart Tolle said in his second book, *A New Earth*, "What you fight against you strengthen, what you resist persists."

If you find yourself in a life experience that is resisting change, take some time to ask yourself some opening questions that may help shift the way you live with change. When did change become an enemy? Why do you fight against it so strongly? Can you control change? Ask these questions and take some time to sit and listen to the messages coming through loud and clear.

For a moment, bring up something that you are resisting. Perhaps it appears as a resentment from the past. Let your thoughts return to the past and observe how justified you feel being resentful. Just watch this and breathe. Remember, this is the past. Is this true now or has something changed? Something has changed. Time has moved onward, the situation or event is no longer present, the wave of change has moved forward. Why then has your emotional and mental body not moved forward? Why do you need to hold onto this resentment? What purpose is it serving?

Take another breath, realizing that indeed things have changed. Reflect upon change as a wave and allow that wave of old resentment to live fully inside, let it get big, visualize the wave becoming huge. Watch it as it reaches its crescendo. Watch it teeter at the very top of the wave.

Hold your breath! How long can you hold it until the wave begins to let go? As you let out your breath, dissolve the old resentment and let it go back into the water. Let the old resentment relax and take a new form as the next wave arises. Observe that you are here in the present moment feeling alive and engaged in your life. Try this over and over with each negative thought that holds you in the past.

You may notice that each successive wave continues to change slightly. Get the hang of change – hang-ten, as the saying goes in the surfing world! Each level and layer of *changeability* becomes easier to ride. The old resentment is dissolving in the wave of change. You are getting free, as you open yourself to other energies and thoughts that have creative potential.

Skillful Means Journal

|3| CYCLES

Change occurs in cycles. Change cycles will bring up certain behavioral patterns in life. In the Medicine Wheel there are Four Cardinal Directions representing four basic cycles. These are: the Southern Direction bringing forth the cycle of learning to trust; the Western Direction which brings forth truth; the Northern Direction that works with discernment; and the Eastern Direction that opens us up to faith/spirituality. Each direction of the Medicine Wheel initially represents a phase of growth. We will look more closely at the attributes and the phases of growth in detail in the coming chapters. Cycles wake up our senses. Cycles are not random; they follow a creative flow in which patterns of awareness emerge.

Let's look at one of the big cycles of life that we are all engaged in living: the decision to incarnate from Source, conception, gestation, birth, childhood, teenager, young adult, adult, mature adult, elder, death, rebirth into Source Light.

Within each of these cycles are spun other cycles, such as the process of moving from childhood to teen, teen to young adult, etc. There are phases and layers and levels of living, learning, loving, doing, and being within each cycle.

There are other types of cycles as well. These show up as behavioral cycles, emotional patterns that have become part of who we are whether they are positive patterns or negative patterns. Negative patterns keep us locked in behaviors that cause suffering and pain, not only with ourself but also with others. Patterns have a life cycle, much like change. We enact them in waves of old past behaviors that we have not resolved, or not become conscious of, yet, but which are coming up constantly so that we can reach a point in our behavioral cycling to recognize that there may be other ways to behave. Other options are open to us.

Within cycles we live behavioral patterns that we have learned; that have been modeled from outside sources such as parents, siblings, teachers, co-workers, society, cultural background; or that we have adopted through our own survival, observation or by choice.

Some of the behavioral patterns we adopt begin in very early childhood. These are the oldest ones and these are behavioral patterns that we take with us into every new cycle of life.

If we repeat destructive behavioral patterns, we block our innate ability to change and grow consciously from cycle to cycle. We are unconsciously recycling emotional, physical, mental and spiritual debris. But this form of recycling does not end up as good compost that will grow something new. It ends up staying within a cycle to be regurgitated again and again until a person makes a decision to change. It is at this point that a miracle occurs. As choice point is reached, a light goes on inside. This is the light of awareness.

Coming to choice point is an act of becoming self-responsible for your life. It is a courageous action that allows the fullness of change to move through your entire being.

SKILLFUL MEANS

Sit quietly either outdoors or by a window looking outside. Quiet your thoughts by taking three deep, centering breaths. Observe a behavioral pattern that is active in your present life. Name it. Observe how the behavioral pattern plays out in your life in cycles. Ask some opening questions: When does it get activated? How do you feel as you repeat the same behavioral cycle? How do you feel after the wave of the cycle has moved through? Breathe and watch the movie of the cycle as though you were watching someone else's life. Just observe and allow insights to arise.

Do not judge your behavior. Breathe and ask the behavior the next clarifying question: What does it need in order to shift? Listen to your inner wisdom voice from a relaxed and quiet state of attentive awareness. Do this exercise while looking out the window or looking at a landscape. Focus your gaze upon the snow, or the grass or a flower. Just observe what is there. As you ask the questions, keep gazing at the natural world. Let your mind relax, opening to your imagination. You are in a resting state of open awareness. You are listening without judging or reacting. You are listening in order to understand the cycle. In doing this, you may hear some surprising answers from the opening and clarifying questions. Journal them.

Let it rest where it is and get on with your day. We know that listening, observing, and allowing the wave of energy to move through with non-judgment alleviates stuck patterns. This allows a cycle or behavior the fullness of the wave.

In retrospect, becoming aware of a cycle loosens its grip as well as your attachment to keeping the old behavior alive. You can let go with ease. The next time the cycle repeats its pattern, you will become aware that it is recycling again, and it will be time to reflect and listen. Each time you do this, you will learn something new and gain insights. Also, you will feel energized and inwardly excited because something is shifting. You are getting free from the old pattern.

Skillful Means Journal

Creations are
   numberless,
I vow to free them.
Delusions are
   inexhaustible,
I vow to transform
   them.
Reality is boundless,
I vow to perceive it.
The awakened way
is unsurpassable.
I vow to embody it.

ZEN BUDDHIST PRAYER

|4| REALITIES

Reality is boundless. Reality is also relative, meaning that it is dependent upon being connected to other things. Reality is truth.

There are seen and unseen realities (truths) related to the physical and spiritual worlds. (In this instance I use the word physical that also incorporates the emotional and mental states of being). For example, the saying; "As above so below" also relates to "As below, so above". From the spiritual perspective, as we grow our soul we are evolving spiritually and this affects our physical experience in the world. The inner spiritual world affects the outer physical world. They are inter-related. Truth is universal and is inter-related to other truths, just as realities are inter-related. When we violate a physical truth, the spiritual world is affected, and vice versa. When a truth is violated in one reality, it affects other realities.

From a spiritual perspective, how could we pollute the earth? We have violated a spiritual truth which is "do no harm to self, others or things". From a physical perspective, how could we deliberately poison our earth? We know the long-term effects of negative actions. And yet, we have become so disconnected from the earth – and from our own physical inter-relatedness with all sentient life – that we arrogantly continue to pollute. The effect is that we have altered the outer physical world, namely the environment of our Mother the Earth. Also, we have trespassed our inner boundaries of balance and peacefulness. One reality is related intimately to the other. We are witnessing the effects of our being out of balance spiritually and physically. We have lost the relationship of spiritual reality to physical reality, which means the laws of cause and effect are being ignored. We are responsible for creating a polluted reality. How do we bring this back into balance? By becoming aware that our thoughts, words, deeds, actions and energy have both a spiritual meaning as well as a physical meaning – all ways!

Grandfather, elder and teacher, and I were talking about the need for the return of humanity's spirituality. He said this, "Human beings have the ability to bring back into balance the wrongs we have done to our Mother the Earth. The creative, scientific technology exits within the human race to change physically what we have harmed and made wrong in our world. The question that remains is whether or not humanity will activate the spiritual side of itself in time to reconnect with the outer world reality and shift our energy back into balance." Both spiritual and physical realities must be engaged consciously. As we evolve in the personal/physical world, so our inner/spiritual understanding expands. Another great wisdom keeper, Mahatma Gandhi said, "Your belief that there is no connection between the means and the end is a great mistake. We reap exactly as we sow." (Gandhi, page *99*, *Voltas Limited*, Navajivum Trust, Vakil and Sons Ltd. Press, Bombay) We are interconnected with all realities.

Everything is energy.
Energy follows thought.
Thought becomes belief.
Belief determines reality.
And reality shapes your destiny.

QUOTE FROM WWW.CHANTAGUA.COM

SKILLFUL MEANS

Take a conscious walk. Fold your hands in front of your mid-section, arms relaxed, shoulders down, back straight, chin parallel to the ground, eyes cast down in front of you. Your gaze is soft, your breathing is deep and regular. Now take one foot and place it slowly forward, connecting with the earth. Place the foot heel to ball until it is set flat in front of you. Balance your weight on both feet. Feel your legs, your back, and notice your breathing. Slowly raise the back foot, heel to toe, breathing deeply, bring the leg forward, placing the foot, heel to toe slightly in front of the planted, balancing foot. As you are getting the hang of balancing by consciously walking slowly, begin to open all your senses. Notice your hearing, sight, kinesthetic connection, your feelings, sense of smell and your awareness to physical and spiritual realties as you are making your way along. In the summer time try conscious walking barefoot. Bring your conscious walking to other surfaces, such as a beach, forest floor, grass, concrete, etc. Notice your senses in different environments, at different times of year. As you walk, observe the thoughts that turn your mind, and the cessation of thought as you develop this walking-waking-meditation. You are not going somewhere. The object is not to see how much distance you can cover in a slow walk for 20 minutes. You are developing a state of being that is both physically conscious and spiritually conscious. You are expanding your senses. In doing so, you are inviting other realities to arise, other awarenesses to surface.

Many people tell me that they feel not only energized after this practice, but they feel very spiritually aware on many levels. They also report their mind is clearer, they feel calmer and they remember their insights.

This simple meditation connects realities. As you develop the consciously aware walk, incorporate the insights you receive from it into your daily life. Become consciously aware of all your actions. Become consciously aware of all realities as one smooth continuum. We are aware on physical, emotional, mental and spiritual levels. Realities are not compartmentalized isolated experiences. Realities are boundless. "Everything is energy. Energy follows thought. Thought becomes belief. Belief determines your reality. And reality shapes your destiny." (quote Chautauqua www.chautaugua.com).

Skillful Means Journal

We have the capacity to explore realities, to connect with ourselves, and all sentient life on physical, mental, emotional and spiritual levels. We have the ability to live in many realities simultaneously as we realize our inter-connected nature.

As human beings we also have the unusual ability to explore our *True Self*. The process is to learn from the past, bring this knowledge and understanding to the present to make conscious choices in the *now*. This also means learning about our *False Self*, also known as the Shadow Self. The Shadow Self is who we are *not*. Paradoxically, it is part of us that we keep from consciousness. The Shadow Self lives in a half world in which it recycles old, outdated behavioral patterns. These keep us in a wounded state, recycling the past over and over. The *Bright Shadow* for some relates to "getting-rid-of-something" in terms of behavioral change, or of healing an illness or disease by fixing what is wrong. The *Bright Shadow* is just as powerful in the Western direction as the dark shadow of the *False Self*. The *Bright Shadow* is a part of the *False Self*. It is made up of fantasy thinking disconnected from reality.

The *False Self* presents as states of being fearful, rigid, jealous, a hater and hated, full of blocked emotions, judgmental, untrustworthy, a liar, a professional victim, deadened or numb. The *False Self* is invested in keeping us locked up. It keeps us from fully engaging in life. It develops Masks of idealized self-identification that it presents to the outer world. The Masks keep us isolated and separate from others. Masks are defenses, like a shield of armor, that are energetic forms we create and hold in our energy field. We have the ability to learn about the *False Self* in order to fully embrace our *True Self*. There is tremendous power locked away in the shadowy half-life of the *False Self*. The *False Self* has so much to teach us about the causes of pain and suffering on all levels of life experience. We have the ability to learn from the *False Self*. Choosing to heal in a conscious way requires opening ourselves up to territory we are uncomfortable exploring. Growth, through learning and taking responsibility for our behavior, is a permanent shift towards being consciously aware.

We have the ability to learn every moment and to grow through life experiences with deep understanding. Once the disconnection of the *False Self* is illuminated, healing is possible. Healing the split in the energy fields consciously is desirable because we evolve not only on a personal level but the entire species evolves. We are learning to become more fully human by making the commitment to delve deeply, coming up with nuggets of truth. The *True Self* incorporates the energy released by the *False Self* as it becomes conscious. Unity consciousness does not have a split. Unity consciousness just *is*. Working with the *False Self* to uncover discomfort releases stuck energy, which then becomes available to a conscious state of being. Balance flows with a sense of integrity and honesty.

SKILLFUL MEANS

Uncovering the *False Self*. Bring up a situation in which you became defensive. Feel the energy of your "hackles rising". This is your defense posture arising. Notice how it feels in your physical body. Listen to the voice in your head and the dialogue it is running. Get a sense of how strong the defense is by describing it. What senses does it activate inside? Does it feel sticky, brittle, sharp, syrupy sweet, cold, remote, resentful, arrogant, justified, angry, jealous, attached to a certain way of identifying itself, sad, silent, brooding? What emotions does it bring forth? Describe the *feeling-tone* of the Mask, recognizing this is a familiar state of being rooted in the past. Recognize this as being part of your *False Self* and that a Mask has been activated. It happens in the blink of an eye. If you can, try giving it a name. Notice how much of your energy is attached to it and how much energy it takes to live inside an activated Mask.

Begin to invoke the witness part of yourself. The witness is the one who has the ability to observe from a state of neutrality and non-judgment. Breathe deeply and activate this wise part of you that knows how to observe things. Watch yourself having your reaction, watch how powerful the reaction is. Experience how much energy is required to maintain this Mask. Experience how you feel deep inside.

Ask one question of the Mask. No matter how it has been activated or under what circumstances, ask the Mask where it comes from. Listen and witness the dialogue. We will be working with Masks later in the book in more detail. For now, become aware of some of your Masks and how they become activated. They may be old friends with whom you are very comfortable. The Mask may have helped you survive in the past. Simply begin to imagine what it would be like to live free of defenses. Mask-free. You are learning. Through learning comes understanding and freedom. 🐢

Skillful Means Journal

|6| FOUR DIRECTIONS AND FOUR DIMENSIONS

There are four aspects of being human that we will engage as we learn skillful means for personal transformation. These aspects are part of our energy fields, known as bodies; The Spiritual Body, The Physical Body, The Emotional Body and The Mental Body. The four aspects are related to The Medicine Wheel in Four Cardinal Directions, each direction having attributes and gifts for conscious awakening.

THE SPIRITUAL BODY – The Eastern Direction, the element is fire. It is the direction of creation. It represents light and The Source Light, illumination, creativity, passion, spirituality (not religion), visions and long-view (or the ability to see long distances). The sense this awakens inside of us is that of inner spaciousness, inner connectedness; an interior landscape that is the unique territory of our soul. It has been known as the direction visionaries and prophets have mastered. The Eastern Direction is the root home of faith.

Faith is belief based upon trust, truth, and discernment. Faith needs no proof of existence. Faith is a state of being.

SKILLFUL MEANS

Reflect upon what faith means for you. Where is faith present in your life? Has there ever been a time when you leaned into (relied upon) faith to get you through difficult times? Reflect upon those times and insights. Where is faith absent in your life? In what ways are you choosing to grow faith in you life now?

the east direction

O Great Spirit of the East,
Radiance of the rising Sun,
Spirit of new beginnings,
O Grandfather Fire,
Great nuclear fire – of the Sun.
Power to see far, and to
Imagine with boldness.
Power to purify our senses,
Our hearts and our minds.

We pray that we may be aligned with You,
So that your powers may flow through us,
And be expressed by us,
For the good of this planet Earth,
And all living beings upon it…

FROM RALPH METZNER'S POEM ON THE *FOUR DIRECTIONS*
(PAGE 134, EARTH PRAYERS)

Skillful Means Journal

_____

_____

_____

_____

_____

_____

_____

_____

_____

_____

_____

_____

_____

_____

_____

_____

the south direction

O Great Spirit of the South,
Protector of the fruitful land,
And of all green and growing things,
The noble trees and grasses,
Grandmother Earth, Soul of Nature
Great power of the receptive,
Of nurturance and endurance,
Power to grow and bring forth
Flowers of the field,
Fruits of the garden.

We pray that we may be aligned with You,
So that your powers may flow through us,
For the good of this planet Earth,
And all living beings upon it…

TO CONTINUE WITH RALPH METZNER'S POEM ON THE *FOUR DIRECTIONS*
(PAGE 134, EARTH PRAYERS)

THE PHYSICAL BODY — The Southern Direction, the element is earth. It is the direction of birth and growth. It represents the physical body of our Mother the Earth, our personal physical body and the physical world. It also represents how connected we are to Mother Earth, and our being personally aware of our behavior, responses and actions. The senses it awakens within us are those of being in relationship with self and others in grounded, practical and honest ways. The Southern Direction is the root home of trust.

Trust is based upon an inner sense of being grounded. Some elements of trust are honesty, integrity, reliability, and self-awareness.

SKILLFUL MEANS

What is your relationship with trust? Reflect upon whether you feel you are a trusting person? Reflect upon times in your life in which you have had to trust someone or yourself during a challenging life experience. In what ways are you choosing to grow trust in your life now? Journal your awareness about your relationship with trust.

Skillful Means Journal

THE EMOTIONAL BODY – In the Western Direction the element is water. It is the direction of the emotional worlds, and of transformation. We grow and mature in the Western Direction. It is also the direction of the Shadow Lands, death, dissolution, letting go, surrender and dismemberment of the past. The Western Direction brings up the hidden lessons of life. The sense it sparks is to "wake up from the trance you are living". In awakening, become fully engaged in the world by accepting your gifts. The watery world of the West is also about delving into the subconscious to find the undercurrents of emotions that need to be brought to the surface for truth to be revealed. The subconscious does not have a filter. Any message the mind thinks the emotional body accepts directly into the subconscious.

Trance-states reside in the subconscious. They are activated from a very power energy field. *Trance states* are how we lull ourselves into a state of self-numbing. Bringing them up to the surface is the process of awakening from the trance. A *trance-state* differs from a Mask, although both are the work of the Western direction. A Mask is a defensive energy field. It has the quality of being rigid. A Mask is enacted with purpose and intention. A trance is much more subtle, although it is born out of a need for survival and safety. The trance also keeps us distant and separated from our *True Self*. The quality of a *trance-state* is like being in a fog. Part of you is aware of what is taking place around you but you are disengaged emotionally. We will be working extensively with waking up from the trance, as well as with defensive Masks in other chapters of the book.

A quote from Grandfather on the work of the Western direction, "It is easy to wake up, the tricky part is staying awake!" The West is "the heart cracked wide-open", of naming the Truth.

the west direction

O Great Spirit of the West,
Spirit of the Great Waters,
Of rain, rivers, lakes and springs
O Grandmother Ocean,
Deep matrix, womb of all life.

Power to dissolve boundaries,
To release holdings,
Power to taste and to feel,
To cleanse and to heal,
Great blissful darkness of peace.

We pray that we may be aligned with You,
So that your power may flow through us,
And be expressed by us,
For the good of this planet Earth,
And all living beings on it…

TO CONTINUE WITH RALPH METZNER'S POEM ON THE *FOUR DIRECTIONS*
(PAGE 134, EARTH PRAYERS)

Truth is the root of all experience. The qualities of truth are integrity, honesty, intention and, facts. Truth is the awareness of being aware in the present moment.

SKILLFUL MEANS

Reflect upon a story you tell yourself or often repeat in life such as, "life is hard but what can you do?" or, "I'm just one little person, how can I make a difference?" or, "No matter how hard I work, I can never get ahead" or, "if only…", or " I wish it were different…" In this reflection, we are identifying an active *trance-state* that you are living. Name just one trance and write it down as a statement.

Trances feel very old, sometimes comfortable; often they are unconscious language that we use every day to describe an experience of our emotional body expressed in thoughts and actions. Trances often feel restricting and make us feel emotionally distant or foggy – as though we can't quite get a handle on something. Find a trance you are living and identify the statement it is recycling.

Ask yourself a few opening questions: How old is this trance, where does it come from? How attached am I to living with it any longer? Is this trance really true? Breathe as you sit in a relaxed state observing the trance as it plays out in your life. Watch the movie of the trance as you live it. Take four deep, cleansing breaths. Bring the breath to the trance state in your emotional body. Imagine each breath as a clear cup of water you are drinking. Visualize the water washing over the bumpy emotional field, softening it, opening up your awareness to what lies underneath the *trance statement*. There is a nugget of something waiting for you to recognize it.

Skillful Means Journal

In the final breath, pick up a pen to write the truth of what lies underneath the *trance-statement* you have identified. Observe this and still breathe. You have uncovered a truth in your life. You are awake to it now.

Allow it space. Truth, once named, can never be buried again. Wisdom from Gandhi, page 177, "Silence is a great help to a seeker after truth. In the attitude of silence the soul finds the path in a clearer light and what is elusive and deceptive resolves itself into crystal clearness. Our life is a long and arduous quest after Truth, and the soul requires inward restfulness to attain its full height."

the north direction

O Great Spirit of the North,
Invisible Spirit of the Air,
And of the fresh, cool winds,
O vast and boundless Grandfather Sky,
Your living breath animates all life.
Yours is the power of clarity and strength,
Power to hear the inner sounds,
To seep out the old patterns,
And to bring change and challenge,
The ecstasy of movement and the dance.

We pray that we may be aligned with You,
So that your powers may flow thorough us,
For the good of this planet Earth,
And all living beings on it.

TO CONTINUE WITH RALPH METZNER'S POEM ON THE *FOUR DIRECTIONS*
(PAGE 134, EARTH PRAYERS)

THE MENTAL BODY – In the Northern Direction the element is air. It is the direction of the mind, of the ego. Paradoxically, it is also the direction of developing mental discernment and wisdom. The mind appears as both the little *I am* thinking mind (the proverbial gerbil on the never-ending squeaky wheel of thoughts), as well as the expanded mind, in which the personality is not engaged. The expanded mind is the witness. This aspect of the mind is able to discern, rather than judge. The mind is adaptable and multi-layered. Remember the famous Lily Tomlin statement about the mind: "The mind is like a parachute; it only works when it is open."

At the same time as holding the state of being as witness, the mind can also be the negotiator/navigator, living whatever experience is in the moment, asking alert insightful questions that support an awakened state of conscious awareness. The work of the Northern Direction is to learn how to get in under the radar screen of the ego in order to be free from attachments. We can retrain the mind with an assigned role of alert, engaged observer in the present moment.

SKILLFUL MEANS

Choose an event from the past that still activates you. Draw a triangle upon a piece of paper. At one angle write the word *witness*. At another angle, write down the word *inquirer*, and at the top of the triangle write the word *experiencer*. Each one of theses states of mind has a role. The witness is neutral with no agenda. The witness is observing actions without attachment. The *inquirer's* role is to ask questions that expand awareness and bring forth discernment. The questions are open ended, creating an alchemical catalyst for conscious awareness. The *experiencer* is living inside the event with cords

Skillful Means Journal

that are directly connected to the past, having old reactions to whatever is happening at the moment, recycling old patterns.

To wake up inside the experience, first breathe and recognize the experience as familiar, uncomfortable, foggy (*trance-state*), defensive (Mask), or as something new. Listen to the thoughts that are turning in your mind. Employ the witness aspect of your mind to step back and observe the experience as it plays out. Allow your intuition to get curious as you observe yourself having an experience while you are having emotional reactions. Ask an open-ended question about the experience, such as, "Where is this coming from?" Allow the insight to arise through the *experiencer*. When you get it, move into the present with the next question, "What is here now?" Is there anything to be gained once you see where the reaction has come from in this present moment? Use the questioning part of yourself to gain insight and update the subconscious and the ego. Is there anything new here? If not, we thank the experience and move onto something present. Insight practice allows the wave of the experience to be felt, recognized, met, listened to and moved forward in time to the present moment. The ego mind can be free from the past.

Discernment is the lesson of the Northern Direction of the mind. The senses engaged in discernment are insight, understanding, recognition, perception and observation in a relaxed state of awareness. Discernment brings us to clarity and peace.

The Four Directions and the life lessons that they bring to us are interconnected and inter-related.

They fit together like pieces of a puzzle that simultaneously give us clues for awakening, as well as support us as we grow our soul. We will be working more with the attributes and the gifts later in the book.

|7| CAPACITIES/POTENTIALS

We have the capacity to accept other realities – to respond to dreams, visions, ideas, creativity and spiritual teachings. The non-material world is an exploration into the unknown. We are part of the unknown, also termed non-ordinary reality. It is available to us when we are open, connected and in a relaxed state of conscious awareness.

"Transformation is an inside job", a quote that is in the collective consciousness now that focuses on the inner work that we are being called to do. Transformation from the inside out is the capacity to reach our true potential. We do this by developing spiritual capacities through engaging in meditation, prayer, awe, wonderment, miracles, visions and dreaming. Connecting to the support provided from the spirit world and from the natural world are all pathways in this journey that open us to greater aware-ness. The ability to ground spirituality in this reality is the balance we are seeking between the outer physical world and the inner spiritual world.

Capacity is our ability to respond to the call to go inward. Capacity has within it the sense of being flexible and open, of conscious choice based upon Trust, Truth, Discernment and Faith. We need to understand and accept that there are worlds and dimensions beyond our ken (our normal understanding). In the spirit world there is a sense known as volition. Volition means to take a step into the unknown, to fly, to make a decision to go forward, not knowing the outcome. Anyone who makes the commitment to change will be aided by the unseen forces of the spirit world. There are guides, teachers, ancestors, mentors – all are allies that appear during times of change, times of risk taking and transformation. These allies appear as both friendly support and as challenge-teachers. An ally provides support and insight along the path. A challenge-teacher may appear as a hard lesson, a contrary person, an event or experience that changes the course of your life. Once you commit to change, the entire unseen world is accessible to you. You have protection each step of the way both in the physical world and the spiritual world.

The only source of failure on a journey is *falling asleep* – going back into the *trance-state* or defensive state (Mask) of the past and staying there. This is known as a regression to the past but at any moment you also have the incredible choice to wake up again, to continue the journey of transformation. The ego-mind is no longer in charge when you commit to living your true potential.

SKILLFUL MEANS

Reflect upon your allies in the physical world and then upon whom you may call in the spirit worlds for help and support. What are your spiritual beliefs?

Begin to describe the gifts you have from within your being. Begin with some opening questions: What gifts do I bring to my life and to the world? For example: Am I naturally funny, or naturally compassionate to animals, etc? Look at the natural capacities you bring into life as positive gifts. Reflect upon a life larger than your personal world, a larger world in which you are bringing your gifts. Often times we can see how we are giving to our outer world before we sit to reflect upon our inner self. Natural capacities are gifts we are born with. They are spiritual gifts we have brought forward to this time so that we may learn, grow and evolve. Make a list of positive ways you are connecting with your potential. Make this list as long as you can, go into detail. Do this for several days. This is a list of your potential. We are *taking stock* in this skillful means practice. The capacity for self-reflection (inward connection and acknowledgment) allows your true potential to come forward. Once you have completed your list take some time to be grateful.

Skillful Means Journal

| 8 | PARTICIPATION/ENGAGEMENT

"I have not conceived my mission to be that of a knight-errant wandering everywhere to deliver people from difficult situations. My humble occupation has been to show people how they can solve their own difficulties." (Gandhi, page 178)

We are each responsible for showing up and participating in the unfolding of our personal gifts. One of the teachings of *The Grandmothers Who Counsel the World*, by Carol Schaefer is that each of us has a responsibility to use our gifts, meaning each person must activate their potential. The ability to engage comes from our intention and commitment – our capacity to say *yes* to participating in life. We can depend upon opportunities that will be presented to us in life so that we can wake up to our potential.

How we respond to opportunities and engage with them is a choice to participate or not. For example, many people do deep spiritual *life-changing* work but fail to integrate it or activate it in meaningful ways. They sit on the sidelines letting others do the larger work of the world.

To engage in life and be in relationship with all sentient life is a choice. We are living in times when creatively thinking outside the box is absolutely required of us in order to change the way we relate to our environment, as well as on many other issues such as health care and education, to name a few. This means that being passive, letting others *fix* the problems we have created is not helpful for our evolution. It is time to *live large* – engage in a life that has meaning in terms of being in service for others, for our earth, for the next seven generations who will come after us. Participation and engagement are a call to spiritual and physical activism. Experiencing daily living as your spiritual practice is engaging at a deep level of change. Many people think that they have to take time out in order to have a spiritual practice. They view spiritual practice as separate from daily life. It is exactly the opposite. Every moment is a spiritual practice, every action can arise from true potential if we bring our conscious awareness to it in this way.

SKILLFUL MEANS

Choose one of your natural capacities from the previous skillful means practice that you feel you have not developed fully in your life. Or perhaps dust off an idea or a project that you put aside "until you had more time". Reflect upon how you are engaged in your life at this time. Are there ways you hold back from fully participating? Reflect upon holding back. What are you waiting for? Ask for dreams, a vision, or spiritual direction on ways to activate your potential. Listen carefully and keep inquiring until you feel you have come to some clarity or an idea begins to formulate. Make a commitment to actively manifest this and begin to do it. Take a risk – do it anyway. As Gandhi says, "Be the change you wish to see in the world." In doing so, we unleash huge amounts of creative energy and inspiration into our environment. Witness the world change as we take charge of our destiny by creatively participating in it.

Skillful Means Journal

_____
_____
_____
_____
_____
_____
_____
_____
_____
_____
_____
_____
_____
_____

The sense that patience teaches us is the ability to wait and maintain steadiness while waiting.

Patience arises from the heart, from the ability to be in a compassionate, neutral state – the witness. Patience does not have an agenda, nor a timetable. Patience just *is*. Patience is experienced as an inner state of spaciousness. Patience is a paradox. We must activate doing nothing. It is a state of conscious waiting. Awareness comes when making a choice to wait. Courage arises from your heart. In French 'coeur' means the heart. Courage means to face anything that may be difficult or painful with an open heart. Patience is a spiritual aspect of our being that needs to be nurtured and grown. Within an open heart lies patience and the seeds of peace.

Will is the ability to move energy through the power of discernment to make choices or decisions. Willfulness is the overuse of will. Willfulness is controlling; a *power-over* energy whereby a hierarchy is enforced (those on top, those on the bottom). For example: the misuse of power through greed.

Willingness is the sense of enthusiasm, of creativity and possibilities. Being willing is a state of spiritual conscious awareness. Being willing can also be enacted in the physical world, such as being willing to make peace. Being willing to be in relationship with someone we have been at war with is one of the first acts of peacemaking. It is certainly the first act of peace-making from within. Being willing to be in relationship with yourself reminds me of the famous statement of His Holiness the 14th Dalai Lama, "Peace begins within".

SKILLFUL MEANS

Reflect on how you use your will. What are your favorite/preferred ways to get through a day? Are you constantly doing, going from thing to thing – multi-tasking? How are you unconsciously employing your will? Feel into your body and take a few deep breaths. Connect to your back, your spine – the power base of will in the physical body. Ask your back if it is tired, over-used, out of balance? What does your willful-self need in order to let go for a few moments? Listen, breathe and follow through. Stretch, laugh, go for a walk. Practice a state of *being* for several minutes and then check back in with your willfulness. Have things settled down or shifted?

What is your relationship to patience? Are you aware of being impatient? When does this arise inside you? What part of you gets activated when you become impatient? Consider the next time you feel yourself becoming impatient as a moment to breathe and engage your witness.

As a witness, you can observe everything around you. You can create space and, in so doing, you can actively become aware that there are other possibilities available to you. What are these other avenues of inquiry you might entertain? Allow your heart's song to come forward to guide you.

Skillful Means Journal

|10| COMMITMENT

Commitment is a promise or a pledge that awakens the sense of dedication to a long-term course of action. Commitment requires that you become involved and make an agreement with yourself or others. Remember this, you are never alone on the journey. Your commitment to live in balance is supported by guides, teachers, spiritual protectors and fellow travelers on the journey. A teacher once told me that every experience in your life is given so that your strength and gifts can come forward to meet the situation. The support around you is there for you to lean into and to lean-upon. It is within each of us to ask for help.

SKILLFUL MEANS

Reflect upon an aspect of your life that you have difficulty committing. What are your fears around commitment? Are they real in the present moment, or are they from the past? For example: You have never made a commitment to_____(you fill in the blank). Breathe and let the past be in the past. What if you were to commit to_____and it didn't work out? Are you still whole and are you still on the journey of discovery? What if you committed to something risky and it did work out? How has your life changed?

| 11 | REMEMBERING

The call to awaken is to remember continually who you are. It is easy to wake up...it is *tricky* to stay awake! Remembering is a daily practice. Remembering is the continual call to be in the *now*. One of the primary senses involved in learning to remember ourselves is to slow things down.

The elements of the 9 Rs — (see diagram and meditation in Chapter 7) are essential in developing the art of remembering.

Remembering comes from the memory that this experience has been in your life before. Understand that you have a choice how to work with it in order to grow your soul.

The act of remembering is a call to awaken deep wisdom from your ancestry. What is ancestry exactly? It is every legacy given to us from every single sentient being, our Mother the Earth and, the entire universe. We have vast stores of knowledge available to us from the spirit world. We have vast stores of knowledge and understanding in each cell of the physical body. I have termed this form of remembering *soulular* memory. It arises directly from the *cellular-soulular* part of us that is physical (your historical ancestry and the earth's) as well as, spiritual remembering.

To remember requires cultivating being mindful. The root of the word comes from ancient Latin *memor*, meaning to be mindful, to remind – or call back that which you already know. From a spiritual perspective, it means to call back parts of your soul that have been lost through the course of trauma, shock or grief. In my previous book, *Remembering the Ancestral Soul: Soul Loss and Recovery* I write about the indigenous healing practice of soul retrieval. Soul retrieval is an ancient shamanic form of healing that calls lost or stolen soul fragments back. These soul parts have memory that get rewoven and integrated, bringing a person back to wholeness.

Another form of soul loss (or dismemberment) is the loss of our relation-ship with the natural world – our Mother Earth. The consequence of this form of soul loss is global. We are reaping the impact of the suffering we have caused due to our forgetting we are inter-related with every living being.

It is a commitment to stay awake! Remembering is a daily practice. Remembering is a form of activism. It is a call to heal and be whole. (In the poem on the following page, the act of remembering is powerfully described.)

SKILLFUL MEANS

Go to the chapter in the book that outlines the 9 Rs and practice the medi-tation. Read it out loud to yourself. Observe which of the Rs you may need to learn more about and incorporate into your daily practice.

Journal your insights, creating time and space to integrate them into your life.

THE ANCIENT ONES

From the beginning
We have been with you.
We are the ancient ones
And we remember.

We remember the time when there was only love,
The time when all breathing was one.
We remember the seed of your being
Planted in the belly of the vast black night.

We remember the red cave of deep slumber,
The time of forgetting,
The sound of your breath,
The pulse of your heart.

We remember the force of your longing for life,
The cries of your birth
bringing you forth.
We are the ancient ones
And we have waited and watched.

You say you cannot remember that time
That you have no memory of us.
You say you cannot hear our voice
That our touch no longer moves you.
You say there can be no return
That something has been lost,
That there is only silence.

We say the time of waiting is over.
We say the silence has been broken.
We say there can be no forgetting now.
We say listen.

We are the bones of your grandmother's grandmothers.
We have returned now
We say you cannot forget us now
We say we are with you
And you are us.
Remember Remember..

PATRICIA REIS, 1995, PRINTED WITH PERMISSION.
REMEMBERING THE ANCESTRAL SOUL: SOUL LOSS AND RECOVERY, BY JANE ELY, D. MIN., AUTHOR HOUSE, 2005

Skillful Means Journal

When we follow a life filled with spirit, the energies of awakening, practice, focus and remembering ourselves becomes second nature. The ancient Buddhist bodhisattva (sage and awakened being), Shantideva said: "Let me be the doctor, the nurse and the medicine to heal all suffering until all sentient life is free."

The Wheel of Life is a reflective mirror to show us our past, the present and to create the future we wish to live. I believe that many young people are in despair because they cannot imagine a positive future. It is our job to find our potential and to come out of hiding to take action so that we can engage our gifts and make a bridge to the future for our children. In order to do this we must take action for the wrongs we have passively condoned or participated in and change them. This means to take responsibility for the past mistakes we have made and to shift our behavior with right-action.

The Wheel of Life assists us in finding the life qualities we need to develop in order to create a world in balance. We must do this first within ourselves and then take it out into the family, community and the world. When you can experience yourself from a stance of loving kindness, then you can perceive others in the same way. When we are connected we have the ability to take action in ways appropriate to the call.

By choosing examples from your life and by reflecting on the Medicine Wheel you will see deeply into your sacred human heart, your true nature. Development on all levels of the wheel never stops. The teachings are in a circle to represent the continuation of life. The greatest teaching of the Wheel of Life is to achieve balance. We can also utilize the Medicine Wheel to mark our progress, to help us define goals and utilize skills with which to live.

Visualize yourself in the center of the wheel, not as a "Southern child" or a "Northern mature adult". Connect from the center outward. When you stand in the center of the wheel and look around at the many lessons and practices of awakening this ancient vessel of wisdom provides, you get a sense of where you need to begin.

We can utilize the patterns in nature and the elements they bring to us. Nature and all natural elements are our teachers; they reflect back to us and help us to awaken. We can utilize the wheel and its attributes to help us experience interconnectedness.

SKILLFUL MEANS

Honor each day upon awakening. Give gratitude for everything in your life – the grace and the challenges. Reflect upon the miracle of life. Find a poem or a prayer that expresses love, compassion, or beauty. Or create your own poem; a sketch or painting that expresses beauty. If you are not artistic, look through a National Geographic Journal to connect with the power of compassion, the majesty of nature, the abundance of Mother Earth. Soak in the magnitude of that element that speaks to you. Place this image in your heart. Receive.

It is my hope that each of you will take these teachings and create your personal mandala that supports you in your life. Being on the path is the journey of awakening. Use discernment; take the teachings expressed here that resonate with you and create a new wheel for your personal reflection and transformation.

Skillful Means Journal

"Grandfather Great Spirit
All over the world the faces of living ones
are alike.
With tenderness they have come up out
of the ground.
Look upon your children that they may
Face the winds and walk the good road to
the Day of Quiet.
Grandfather Great Spirit
Fill us with the Light.
Give us the strength to understand,
and the eyes to see.
Teach us to walk the soft Earth as relatives
to all that live."

SIOUX PRAYER
(EARTH PAYERS, PAGE 184)

3

THE MEDICINE WHEEL OF LIFE

mapping consciousness: the seven sacred directions

Within each direction
are gifts and shadow elements.
This next section
of the book details each
of the Seven Sacred Directions.

| INTRODUCTION | There are Four Cardinal Directions of the Medicine Wheel that hold energies relating to the foundation of the elements, Earth, Water, Air and Fire plus The Above Direction, Father Sun, Mother Moon and Star Nations; The Below Direction, The Elementals of Earth's Intelligence and The Devic Kingdom; and the Central Direction, Balance, Harmony and The Sacred Heart of Wisdom. Altogether there are Seven Sacred Directions. The Semi-Cardinal Directions, between each of the Cardinal points of S, W, N and E are the South East, the South West, the North West and the North East. They hold the medicines of shifting consciousness and change relating to initiation, transformation and transmutation. *See graphic on page 26-27.*

| CENTER OF THE WHEEL | Place of balance, harmony and soul life lessons (soul blueprints). The Center holds the soul's decision to incarnate from other realities into this earth walk from conception to birth. Known as the *now place* in the Medicine Wheel, it represents our ability to receive and give in balance. Being receptive allows the gifts of abundance and flow. From the place of receiving and of self-nurturance, we are able to give. We cannot give from a deficit position of being drained or overwhelmed. The Shadow of the Center of the Wheel is "it is better to give than to receive." Many cultures have this belief. Another Shadow part of this belief is that when you give, you receive. In balance, this is partially so. Out of balance over-giving creates co-dependency and over-responsibility for others. The reverse is actually true. When we give cleanly and with clarity from a place of self-empowerment, we are in balance because we are coming from an awareness of already being fulfilled.

the south east direction

Place of new beginnings,
new discoveries, birth and endings.
Birth and death/regeneration,
recalibration, it represents a
change-transmutation cycle.

the south direction

| THE PHYSICAL BODY |

The South is home;
Mother Earth home,
home to self,
home with body wisdom,
home with the divine feminine.

THE GROUND OF BEING

| THE PATH/CYCLES | The beginning of life lessons as an infant and child, from birth to teenager. Learning about the physical body, growing the body and our awareness with early relationships. Our relationship to mother, father and the natural world is emphasized in this cycle. We develop our ground of being which is crucial for all other life experiences. In subsequent cycles around the Medicine Wheel, this direction brings us back to the physical body and what needs to be attended to such as health. Without being grounded other aspects of awakening cannot take root.

| ATTRIBUTES | Trust, love, innocence, wonder, openness, being grounded, safety

| AFFLICTIONS | Wounds and wounded nature through childhood experiences. The loss of attributes or the erosion of attributes through disempowerment from outside sources. The child loses the ability to self-reference and feel safe. The wounds of the Southern Direction have life long implications for healing and self-conscious awakening. The wounds recycle throughout life until the person comes to choice point, deciding to be responsible for personal growth. The wounds are: *pre-verbal* terror, the infant does not stay in the physical realms – takes refuge out of body; *abandonment*, the young child believes itself to be unlovable; *invasion-lack of individuation*, the child is subjected to passive aggressive parenting – withdraws to get away; *betrayal*, the youngster is over powered, lied to/or seduced; *isolation*, the child separates from self and others by maintaining a protective rigid exterior. *See Masks in chapter 8.*

element

| MOTHER EARTH |

The wounds are covered over with Masks known as defenses. Underneath every Mask is a *trance-state*, a hypnotic belief that keeps recycling patterns and experiences.

| ELEMENT | Mother Earth

| COLOR | Red

| FORM | Trust. The Body – the physical world

| TIME | The Big South Moon time is from birth through age 6.9-9.0.
See other Big Moon Cycles, Chapter 6.

| THE JOURNEY | Development of positive will. 1st/2nd/3rd chakras; life force energy, finding the ground/earth, basic trust. Ground develops first before opening to expanded energies. Finding simplicity, openness, reconnecting with the natural world and with self. Learning to trust self.

| SPIRIT ANIMAL HELPERS & THEIR MEDICINE |
Serpent
Has the ability to shed old skins and outmoded behaviors, continual growth through ongoing initiations. Snake is the wise elder of the below world, representing the return of the divine feminine in global psyche, the goddess figure of power and mystery.

Turtle

In Native American Indian creation stories, turtle balances Turtle Island (North America) upon her back. Turtle represents our mother the earth. Grounded and safe, posses ancient wisdom of the earth. Associated with longevity, patience, and skill. Sensitive to vibrations, exceptional perception abilities. Uses higher senses to discriminate what you can trust, who you can trust.

Coyote

The playful trickster, holds up the mirror for self-examination. Helps you learn to laugh at yourself and your behaviors. Messes up the *mind-field* when we get too serious, coyote brings forth humor and helps us learn to adapt.

Mouse

Moves into small spaces with ease, curiosity, scrutiny. Has the ability to look at things up close, never misses details, uses sharp focus to pay attention to details.

| QUESTIONS | What do I need to become aware of in order to heal my body? Is there anything coming up in my life at this time for deeper self-examination? Any patterns that I am uncomfortable with? If so, what Mask do I need to work with? What *trance-state* is underneath the Mask from the past? What skillful means can I practice to move from the past into the present?

| CHALLENGE | Fear (activates wounds) underneath the wound are the *trance-states*; fear tells us to wake up. Fear is ongoing in the wheel of life. It gets replayed until we clarify consciously and are no longer activated by old reflexive behaviors. The challenge is to become free!

| WOUNDS | Childhood wounding, abuse, neglect, not enough, no constancy, abandonment by parent(s). Lack of individuation process; developmentally frozen, recycling old stories. Recycling societal/cultural wounds "Be this way in my image…", child becomes powerless as parents live vicariously through child. Fight, flight, survival mechanisms kick-in.

| SHADOW | *Physical health* – how you treat yourself reflects how you treat others and the earth.

The trance is a hypnotic attachment to staying small and helpless. There is a demand that the outer world owes you something. Masks of self-judgment and self-abuse are played out by judging/abusing others. Early addictions are formed, ie. to food, sex, drugs.

| INITIATION | Facing your fears, meeting and accepting them. Turning around to face your patterns is the initiation of "biting the tiger on the nose" insight practice. Initiation into *individuation* unfreezes the childish self that is locked up, learn to self-parent by becoming aware of issues of trust as they arise. Allow the wave of the wound to move through cleanly and clearly.

| GIFT | *Little Boy/Little Girl* – Trust (playfulness) and compassion, openness, grounded in love and safety.

The trusting child has confidence in things as they are and has the ability to carry this through in life. Childlike wonder opens you to possibilities. It dissolves the old patterns.

| SACRED PLANT | *Sage* – transforms energy, cleanses and cuts through negative patterns.

the south west direction

Place of initiation. This aspect of the Wheel
is a change and transformation cycle.
The volition that comes from within creates movement forward.
It is a time of exploration, individuation and
emotional development, curiosity, testing boundaries,
exploring new territory. I call this aspect of the Wheel,
a *Star Trek* "Enterprise" phase. It is a time of taking risks,
going out beyond known territory and
exploring new landscapes, thoughts, beliefs and identities.

the west direction

| THE EMOTIONAL BODY |

Place of introspection
and meeting the self.
Masks and reflected
mirror images of self and our shadow.
The direction represents what is
below the surface of things.
It brings forth the watery world of emotions.

THE EMOTIONAL BEING

| THE PATH/CYCLES | The theme is the emotional world as experienced in personal dynamics, defenses (Masks), repeating negative behavioral patterns *trances-states* from Teenage ages 12.9-15 through to young adulthood. Learning skillful means to work with the *False Self* to become free so that the *True Self* emerges. The maturation process of defining boundaries, maintaining them and learning to face the truth is the path of this cycle. Self-image, personal change, and all types of relationships are focuses of the cycle.

| ATTRIBUTES | Truth, boundaries, intuition, growing up, letting go, "the heart cracked wide open", unveiling of self on a deeper level, deep inner work – *know thyself* truth-seeking, and verbalizing the truth.

| AFFLICTIONS | Defenses, attachments to old behaviors, the wounded adult with power issues, addictions, dependencies, the dark shadow represents unresolved emotional content that produces Masks and hypnotic *trance-state*s in which the person becomes enmeshed, loses contact with reality, others and the outer world. Attachment to childhood "stories from the past" with over-dependency on staying stuck, the *trance-state* is fed with more trauma/drama, entrenching past beliefs and images; defenses become stronger and more justified as the adult learns how to manipulate behaviors.

| ELEMENT | Water

| COLOR | Indigo/black or dark blue

element

| WATER |

| FORM | Truth. The emotional world, subconscious becomes consciousness

| TIME | The first Big Moon time in the west is puberty, through teens, ages 12.9-15 yrs.

| THE JOURNEY | Cultivating healing practices that support Witness/ Inquirer/Experiencer model for self awareness. The 3rd, 4th and 5th chakras – sense of self is strong enough to explore emotions and heart to move forward; opening into truth allows the WIE model to unveil the *False Self* so that the *True Self* emerges. The purpose is to be free from the emotional past, from the enmeshment of *toxic story*. There must be a quality of willingness and open heartedness. Learning to access personal power in a balanced way. Learning to speak the truth, (5th chakra) and maintain truth as a reality.

| SPIRIT ANIMAL HELPERS & THEIR MEDICINE |

Jaguar
Insightful energy combined with stillness and power to perceive that which others may not see. The jaguar has the ability to see through illusions.

Bear
Having the heart to go inward, into the subconscious to find the truth. Working with dreams and inner visions to find truth. Bears foster the imagination, provide energy to go deep within, be reclusive in order to nurture self, and then come out with new potentials.

Thunder Beings

Thunder Beings cut through *trance-state*s, help a person wake up and see what is in front of them. Sharp, clear cracks of lightning and thunder bring us power to wake-up, use our senses and grow our soul.

Beaver/Otter

Relationships are important lessons, building community, being playful together. Water element associated with these animals points to healing emotional wounds through repairing the past with skillful means and building a foundation for the future. Beavers are wisdom keepers and dreamers. Otters awaken curiosity and remind us to play.

Raven

Call for justice, calls for the truth, representing memory and stirring up magic in your life without fearing it. Raven sees behind outer appearances to find the true meaning either in a playful way or sometimes as a trickster. Fool or wise master? Raven invites you to come into your life fully.

| QUESTIONS | What defenses (Masks) do I use to keep me from growing? What are the hypnotic trances (beliefs and images) I enact in my life? How can I become free from causing my own pain and suffering? What does my soul need in order to grow? What must I give away to crack open my heart?

| CHALLENGE | Death, dismemberment, dissolving, letting go, living through the dark night of the soul — making the enemy the ally by unveiling the illusions. Dismemberment in order to remember and surrender; unveil yourself to yourself. Coming to memory, coming home to truth.

| WOUND | Behavioral wounds play out as unreceptive, emotionally unavailable, cold/distant, untruths (lies), manipulation (lack of morality) with impunity (gets away with it — no consequences) or as one who gives away inner authority and acts powerless, conversely can be over bearing and invasive.

| SHADOW | Recycling destructive emotional behavior, outwardly displacing it by blaming and shaming others. The unwillingness to do the *False Self* work. Being reactive and causing chaos while running away from personal inner conflict and chaotic emotions. Attachment to *toxic story*, the inability to take responsibility for self and actions.

| INITIATION | Facing sadness and grief due to soul loss. Allowing the heart to crack open, allowing the flow of sadness and stuck emotions. Bringing the grief to the surface, lifting it up and finding out what is underneath it.

Male opens to feminine aspects of self by unveiling illusions, through inviting grief and sorrow – male finds his *intuitive energy*. Female finds her inner warrior, her male aspect – female finds her inner strength, *power*. Both male and female aspects come into balance with *True Self*. True emotion is pure, clean and clear. Grief cleanses the wounds, heals the wounds and begins the healing process.

| GIFT | Acceptance, surrender, greater sense of intuition. Freedom from the past. Male accepts inner feminine self; female accepts her inner male self. In balance this creates a spiritual adult. The gift is also the death of identifying with the past, and identifying with the unconscious *False Self*.

| SACRED PLANT | Cedar; cleansing, seeing into the shadows, cuts through attachments.

the north west direction

Value systems develop; also in the transformation cycle
we enter new territory of the unknown,
it is a maturation process of development
that occurs and a sense of justice develops.
Awe and magic develop with spiritual awakening
and within spiritual practices.
Generally speaking, this aspect relates to developing
a deeper relationship within self to truth and
to communicating and speaking the truth on many levels.

the north direction

| THE MENTAL BODY |

Living with clarity and intention.
The element of the north is the wind.
The wind clears the obscurations
of the mind and brings clarity to thinking.
The maturation process brings forth wisdom,
the ability to witness and
hold clear presence.

THE MIND BODY

| THE PATH/CYCLES | The path of becoming a "true human being" – meaning becoming a mature adult with abilities to respond, rather than to react, maintaining an open heart and an open mind. The greatest ability developed in the North is that of discernment (differs from judgment). The ability to live life as experienced in an undefended way using discernment is the path of the North. It is the home of the ancestors, the wisdom keepers, and the teachers. It is the direction in which we glimpse ourselves as future mentors fully embodying our life tasks, work and play.

| ELEMENT | Air, the four winds

| COLOR | White

| FORM | Discernment. The mental body – the right use of the mind. The intellectual mind, the heart mind, the wisdom mind

| TIME | Entering adulthood to full adult in the first cycle of the medicine wheel, (age 19-21, the Big South Moon cycle).

|ATTRIBUTES| Development of discernment, wisdom, clarity of thought and purpose, serenity, peace, intentional living. Response-ability develops over the reactionary self. *Soul-full* feeling of being content brought on by culmination of good work through good intentions. The observer/witness is in place and able to hold space for life experiences. Healing attributes include: reconciliation, insight, academics, further study, mentorship of young people, and living a consciously aware life.

|AFFLICTIONS| The greatest cause of suffering is the mind's attachments to its thoughts. The ego-mind or "little I am" thinks it is in charge and in control. Often played out as controlling behavior, perfectionism, psycho-pathic behavior, arrogance, power-over others behavior, greed, judging others in the outer world and also judging self, obsessive patterns – outwardly displaced energy leads to others being at fault, or disappointment. Also, a "right of entitlement" can be an affliction if the early child/teen has not encountered appropriate boundaries and positive behavioral models.

|THE JOURNEY| Taming the mind through using skillful means. Under-standing "thoughts have energy", thoughts cause unconscious attachments and grasping behaviors. Learning to take responsibility for your thoughts and for your actions is the conscious journey of transformation, embodying life's lessons and insights (5th Chakra). Working with hypnotic *trance-states* to clear the mind of old patterns is the path of "trance-formation". This path also is the beginning of dreaming a life that is larger than the "little I am"; a future that has a larger world view than the self. Development of the dreamer/mystic self begins, 6th Chakra begins to open.

| SPIRIT ANIMAL HELPERS & THEIR MEDICINE|

Buffalo

The Buffalo (give-away) represents the great horns of balance. Knowing what it means to *give-away* in life, also the dreamer and the Sun Dancer, Buffalo brings balance through prayer and sacredness to the planet and the people. The buffalo is a witness to human beings.

Owl

Night Eagle, is a wisdom-keeper. Owl has the ability to see in the dark, and to see through the dark, sees through shadows and Masks.

Owl balances the realms of spiritual realities and the world of the mind, the innate ability to work with discernment. It is a bird of great power, often seen as messenger, a bringer of omens.

spiritual animal helper

| BUFFALO, OWL, HUMMINGBIRD, DRAGON, COUGAR |

Hummingbird

This tiny bird has great power to traverse great distances without fear of the unknown. It provides an inner wisdom that guides us to where we need to go. It brings beauty and joy into our life.

Dragon

The ancient wisdom from when the earth was being formed remains in our bones and this wisdom is accessible to us and to all beings upon the planet. Dragons bridge ancient knowledge. We can see their descendents walking the earth in the forms of lizards, alligators, crocodiles, snakes, to name a few. Also, mountain ridges, mountain ranges from south to north represent the bones of dragon energy.

Cougar

Learning about your own power. The cougar is a dreamer. Learn to watch your dreams for spiritual wisdom and messages from your soul.

|QUESTIONS| What motivates me in life? What are the predominate thoughts that turn my mind? Beginnings of questioning the mind and the ego. What is the difference between judgment and discernment? How do I practice either of them? What are my intentions…in life, in relationship, in work?

|CHALLENGE| Growing up, growing the soul through experiencing life. Embracing life experiences as teaching moments, the ability to discern and to move forward without getting enmeshed in old outdated thoughts.

Recognition that our thoughts have power and energy. How we think is what we manifest. Learning to go beyond the self-identification of the mind and tap into the larger energies available to us.

|WOUND| Not stepping into your role of being self-responsible. The inability to stay in relationship with self and others, inability to be in right relationship with your actions (selfishness, mental recycling, regressing into old behavior patterns).

|SHADOW| Mental confusion, recycling unconscious *trance-states* and staying powerless, "I don't know how to change", or " I am entitled because…" Religious dogma or cult like indoctrination or beliefs are used as a crutch. Cults, giving away power to gurus, looking outside yourself for transcendental spiritual delivery, all cause *trance-states* to continue. Brain washing through the use of mass media messages, ie. fear is the normal state in which humans must live. Look for these all around you and break the trance when you see them with, " Cancel, clear. This does not belong to me nor to Mother Earth."

Leaving it up to authority power figures to make decisions on your behalf negates being personally responsible. Lack of discernment allows powerlessness and means your energy is *leaky*.

|INITIATION | The initiation is of the mind. In the initiation nothing makes sense, deconstruction of old paradigm values and beliefs allows intellectual defenses (Masks) to crumble in order to break through to inner wisdom. Trance states unwind as Masks dissolve. The sense of coming out

of a trance is powerful. Letting go of intellectualizing. In the stillness that comes cosmic unity awareness arises. Initiation: What it means to be an adult woman; what it means to be an adult man.

| GIFT | Actively listening to your thoughts with non-attachment; discerning truth from fantasy. Sharing inherent wisdom, stepping into the role of teacher, elder, or mentor. Guiding the next generations. Serving the world through embodying your life task. Gratitude practices, being thankful for your life.

Being able to hold the paradox of "both/and potentials" (rather than an either/or mentality that is limiting) – an open mind that witnesses with clarity and non-judgment. This is practiced within self-first, and then with others.

| SACRED PLANT | Sweet grass; a feminine herb that balances our inner female. It represents living in good relationship with spirits and all life.

the north east direction

Shifting attitudes and balance. Clarity and developing vision.
This cycle brings forward hopes, dreams and wishes for the future.
This transformational time brings a sense of deepening awareness
and poignancy in valuing all that life has to offer.
It is a maturation point in the wheel and often is a time
when an individual changes life path or changes directions.
Big transformation cycles happen in North East.

the east direction
| THE SPIRITUAL BODY |

Creativity, farsighted vision,
illumination and manifestation.
This is the path of finding your "YES",
stepping up to the plate
taking action and learning how
to manifest change in your life.
Living a spirit filled life as daily practice,
living passionately, with joy.

THE SPIRITUAL BODY

| THE PATH/CYCLES | In this path you learn to "walk your talk" with support from spiritual helpers, teachers and role models. The path is Faith, learning to have faith, living your faith, acknowledging your self as an empowered person.

| ATTRIBUTES | Engaged spirituality, development of compassion, exploration, creativity and playfulness. Living passionately with a more farsighted world-view. Fire energy fuels visions, visions are manifested through balanced activity. The Eastern Direction is the power of the sun to shine light, to bring the light and to grow the soul, through engaged action, visionary experiences, farsightedness, creativity, illumination and manifestation; 6th and 7th chakras.

| AFFLICTIONS | The greatest cause of pain and suffering in the Eastern Direction is unresolved anger, hatred and resentment. Also, the denial of not being self-responsible. Allowing outer world demands to take precedence over living life as a spiritual adult (being out of balance with inner and outer world). Conversely, a false dependency upon a fantasized spirit world that causes dissociation (a *trance-state*), infantile thinking and actions that put you in jeopardy due to being ungrounded and out of practical reality. "The bright-shadow" being blinded by the light – giving away your power to spiritual teachers, "guru-*trance-states*"; being taken advantage of by spiritual cults with authority figures who control and manipulate often through subtle means or sometimes through greed. "The bright shadow" has also been termed as "new age fallacy".

color
| YELLOW (RISING SUN) |

| ELEMENT | Fire

| COLOR | Yellow (rising sun)

| FORM | Faith. Spirituality (not religion)

| TIME | The first Big South Moon cycle spans from 0 to approximately 27 years, which brings you to your first Saturn Return, (an astrological term meaning a time of rebirth/birth and transformation). It is a time of recognizing positive growth patterns, insights and changes that become available to us. We go through four moon cycles in the medicine wheel of life, each one lasting approximately 27 years. Each time we move from one Big Moon cycle into another, we are in transition and initiation. Our soul's life path is maturing, becoming more clear. *See Medicine Wheel charts for clarification.*

| THE JOURNEY | The act of consciously practicing loving kindness and compassion (Faith - 7th Chakra) towards self and others. Purpose, vision, farsightedness – engaged future potentials are activated in this journey. Perceiving the nature of realities through the use of discernment, insights and dreaming allows the soul to develop a larger world-view. Ceremony becomes part of the spiritual journey to keep you moving forward. The *inquirer* part of your true nature brings up possibilities that fuels manifestation of visions and dreams.

| SPIRIT ANIMALS & THEIR MEDICINE |

Eagle

The eagle brings messages from Great Spirit, gifts of vision to create a world in balance. The practice is long view or farsightedness. Decisions are made understanding the implications of an action for the next seven generations.

Condor

Has the ability of *direct knowing* from Great Spirit. This is an immediate energy of being given a transmission of what is right. It is clarity of vision, an inner spiritual knowing. Condor is a big healing animal spirit that illuminates those places that need attention.

Hawk

Soars and calls you to your soul growth. The hawk, like eagle has sharp vision. It represents being a guardian of power. The hawk cracks open illusions and reveals our inner illusionary Masks so that we can be free.

Butterfly

The energy of transmutation. The butterfly begins as an egg, becomes a caterpillar, goes into deep stillness of the cocoon for internal growth and manifests itself as a winged creature of beauty and fragility. The butterfly teaches us about living with paradox, living as a vulnerable being capable of great things.

| QUESTIONS | In what ways am I holding past resentments and anger? How can I employ skillful means to heal them? If I could imagine myself

free, what would my life be like? How can I learn to lighten up and play? What messages am I transmitting to the world from my behavior? How is the outer world responding to these behaviors? What does faith mean to me on a daily basis?

| CHALLENGE | The misuse of power, distortions of willfulness and intellectual arrogance. Burnout from *trying* too hard and improper use of will. Blind spot is not allowing support and help through spiritual practices. Unconscious stories like "trying and not attaining", "needing and not getting".

| WOUND | This wound has *too much-ness* or an over-powering willfulness to blindly follow a doctrine even if it harms your health. There is a confusion and distortion about what spirituality means. Another wound scenario is an inability to face suffering, pain and abuse. Many people who have intellectually studied and who have not embodied spiritual process can present as a closed energy field. The Mask in this case is "you can't teach me – been there, done that", also known as *spiritual arrogance*. Underneath this is anger and resentment. These are just a few scenarios being enacted.

| SHADOW | Spiritual arrogance; spiritual justification; importance of self image identity rules over spiritual practice. Negative forms are enacted by destructively acting out the "spiritual Mask".

For example: A spiritual leader of a community will cast you out of the community because you do not conform to the will of the leader. Or, a spiritual leader will make you *special* by giving you privileges not granted to others in the community. In a destructive way, this can also lead to

seduction through energy and sexual abuse; also of power over *followers*.
Just one of many ways the Eastern gate of faith can be distorted.

| INITIATION | The fire of passion and creativity must become balanced
with the body, mind, spirit and emotions. The great equalizer is to "walk
your talk" in a humble non-attached, non-grasping open way. The "I can
do it all" Mask must crumble. This is the path of the heart and only the
heart. Your heart, coupled with discernment will lead you.

This is the incorporation of a full cycle of the Medicine Wheel;
integration is part of this process. Time, space and patience to integrate
is part of this initiation.

We so often forget the importance of taking time for integration.

| GIFTS | Vision, openness to psychic abilities, using them in balance and
in the service of others and for spiritual evolution of all sentient beings.
Freedom from the past. Going beyond freedom by being in service for others
and our world. Visions that have long-range potential.

| SACRED PLANT| Tobacco (natural, organic), communication with spirits,
holy smoke given in thanksgiving and honor for all we have been given.
Honoring our ancestors and their teachings.

|ABOVE DIRECTION| Celestial Beings whose task is to be with Mother Earth and all her beings as we evolve. Celestials are Angelic Beings, Council of Light Beings, Ascended Masters, as well as Star Nations Beings whose attributes are wisdom, teachers, peacemakers, earth keepers, inter-galactic beings who have the highest and best good for all sentient life on Mother Earth within their consciousness.

|BELOW DIRECTION| The Devic Kingdom, (the elemental intelligent beings of the earth). The elements of Earth, Water, Air, Fire and Space. The Subterraneans and other intelligent beings that exist below the surface of Mother Earth.

|CENTER DIRECTION| Balance and harmony. The sacred heart of compassion and understanding. In the Center Direction our soul's blueprints (Life Lessons) are grounded, awaiting our choice to bring them forward into consciousness. Free will and free choice are a unique human attribute on our planet. How we exercise these choices brings us into balance or out of balance. "Being in Balance" activates coherency, harmony, inclusivity, co-operation and peace. "You are here to enable the divine purpose of the universe unfold. That is how important you are." (quote by Eckhart Tolle)

4

THE MEDICINE WHEEL OF LIFE
a mandala for awakening

Attributes and lessons
to discover in working
with the Medicine Wheel.

Now we will do a reflective exercise that brings you into the Medicine Wheel. After having experienced the first twelve teachings, The Seven Sacred Directions and the semi-cardinal points of transition of the Medicine Wheel, reflect upon a direction that has the most meaning for you. Or look at the teachings that opened up a new awareness, whether in your body sensations, your thinking, emotional insights or on a spiritual level. Go back to read your journal, insights and dreams from the first twelve skillful means exercises. Then look at the graphic of the medicine wheel and hook this up with the meanings of the Seven Sacred Directions. See if you can find a position or direction of the wheel that calls to you. Imagine yourself walking into a stone medicine wheel, a standing circle created by the ancient ones, to sit in a medicine place for your healing. Visualize yourself sitting down in that direction. How does it feel?

Then review the synthesized teachings below. Read them out loud. As you do, allow the words to flow over you and through you.

part one

THE QUALITIES AND TEACHINGS OF THE WHEEL OF LIFE

| 1 | In the most general of senses, the Medicine Wheel opens you for self-discovery and healing. It provides a model upon which you can explore life experiences, connecting the dots with understanding and insight.

| 2 | It is a place from which to begin to awaken from the past, learning to live in the present and learning to imagine (dream) the future.

| 3 | The Medicine Wheel will support and assist you in unraveling the truth of how you are living your life. It will show you places where you need to focus.

| 4 | It shows us life cycles providing insights into these phases as we traverse the Wheel of Life: birth, childhood, teenager, young adult, mature adult, young-elder, elder, death.

| 5 | Being a circle, the Medicine Wheel is emptiness and fullness simultaneously. It teaches us the paradox of everything and nothing, grasping and non-attachment, and of the absolute principle truth that everything is impermanent.

| 6 | It teaches us that there are many realities and that conscious awareness arises when practicing being an observer, asking yourself open ended questions to inquire about the experience you are having; also known as The Witness, Inquirer, Experiencer, model. It also teaches that we are inter-related with all life.

| 7 | It shows us rites of passage in different phases of development in our life – that to fully embody a rite of passage means to live a spiritual practice, daily.

| 8 | It is a model with skills or tools for coming into balance, awakening, shifting behaviors, strengthening awareness and healing.

| 9 | It opens pathways that are non-linear, to inner landscapes and other realities.

The Medicine Wheel offers a rich world of spirit helpers and teachers to support and guide us on the journey. The wheel is circular and therefore cannot be used in a linear thought process. It opens us up to the webbing of life as we learn how to access the teachings.

| 10 | It brings us into accepting life the way it is through being grounded and grateful, by living in the present moment.

| 11 | Working the Medicine Wheel helps you question your assumptions, and it shakes up rigid thoughts, beliefs and behavioral patterns. The endless (tiring) stories we use to keep us stuck in the past are dissolved when we drop the mantel of resistance to change.

| 12 | It provides compassionate support for individuation and soul growth. It provides a supportive webbing to create balance and harmony in your life. A universal truth states: "As one grows, so do we all." As you grow, you are growing conscious awareness globally.

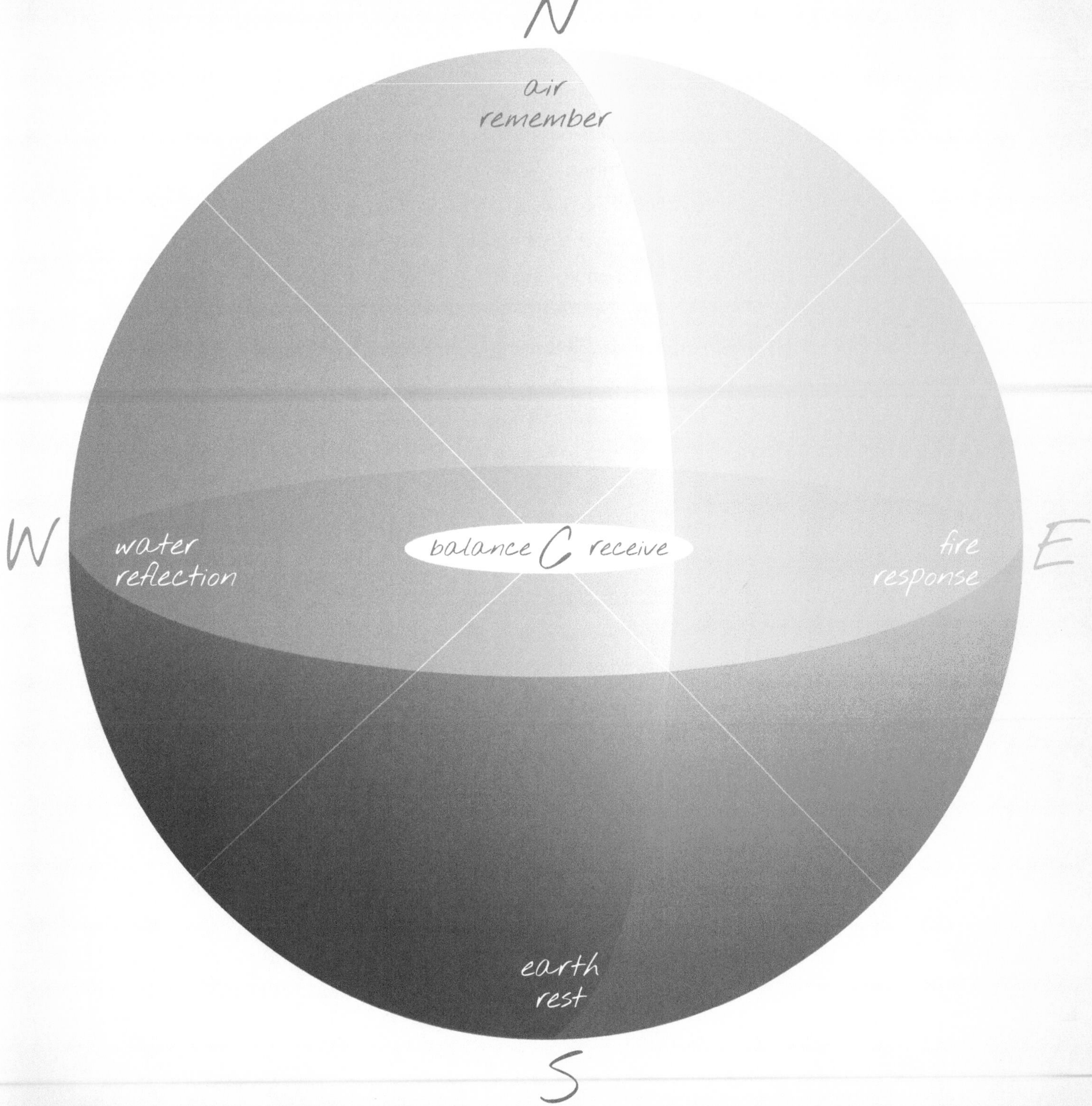
N
air
remember
W
water
reflection
balance C receive
fire
response
E
earth
rest
S

part two

Imagine you are still sitting in the direction of the Medicine Wheel that you have chosen. Look at the graphic of The Seven Sacred Directions and their initial attributes, for example: The Western Direction attributes are truth, the emotional world, introspection, self-reflection, shadows, the element is water; the color is black. Then look across the circle to the opposite direction you are facing. In this example you are sitting in the West looking towards the East. Eastern Direction attributes are faith, spiritual practice, illumination, creativity, passion, vision, the element is fire; the color is yellow.

The place you are sitting in *represents the attributes that you seek*, your soul is calling you to work with, (there is a resonance within you that calls you to this direction.) The spot you have chosen offers medicine for you to awaken and explore. The *place across the circle* you are facing represents the *challenges* you will meet as you work in the present direction. For example, as you work with your emotional world, you will be challenged by your spiritual faith to illuminate or bring light to the emotional shadows of the West that need to be healed.

Skillful Means Journal

The attributes beside you in the Medicine Wheel (in this example the South West is at your right side, as you sit in the West) represents energies that support you in the work you are doing in the particular direction. The *attributes* in the South West are initiation and change which means a *testing* time with energetic support to move forward.

The attributes in the North West, as you sit in the West represents *gifts* that you will use in the work of the direction you are sitting in. North West represents clarification of values and integrity. This supporting energy carries justice and universal truth. In working with your emotions you will lean upon the *attributes* of the South West and the North West to support you as you stay in the direction and work with it.

As we go through the many layers of the Medicine Wheel keep the opposite/challenge attribute and the beside/ally attribute and the gift attribute in mind. Revisit this often throughout working with the many different Medicine Wheels in the book and the exercises.

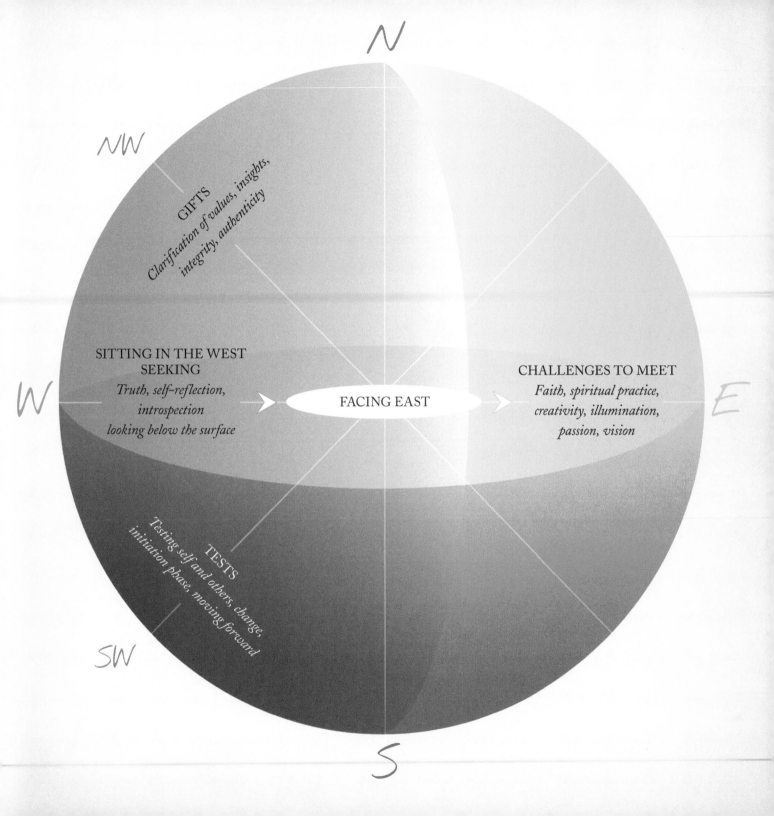

N

NW

GIFTS
Clarification of values, insights,
integrity, authenticity

SITTING IN THE WEST
SEEKING
Truth, self-reflection,
introspection
looking below the surface

W

FACING EAST

CHALLENGES TO MEET
Faith, spiritual practice,
creativity, illumination,
passion, vision

E

TESTS
Testing self and others, change,
initiation phase, moving forward

SW

S

The Seven Causes of Illness

The Wheel of Life offers us tremendous opportunities for self-discovery, healing and growth. As a species upon Mother Earth there are many impediments and obstacles that can keep us stuck in ignorance and complacency. The most difficult veil for human beings to break through is the veil of resistance to change. As a word smith, I look at the word veil and the energy that shrouds it from consciousness. When the letters are rearranged it becomes the word evil. As we break through the veil of resistance, ignorance and complacency we have activated our true potential. All avenues, capacities and potentials open when we find a crack in the netting that shrouds our inherent intelligence. How Masks get played out in our behavior is part of the Seven Causes of Illness. Our Masks (or defenses) feed into "who we are not", and thus feed into resistance, ignorance and complacency. *Trance states* cause a fog or a sleepiness. Trances dissolve our free will and free choice. Trances are underneath each Mask. The trance is a state of disempowerment that locks us in redundant re-enactments of self-destructive behaviors. *See the Addendum and Exercises on Masks.*

The gridlock netting surrounding our collective energy field constricts our consciousness from breaking through. It can be described in relationship with the Medicine Wheel and the Seven Causes of Illness. Have hope; this is about to change because you are signing up to shift it, NOW!

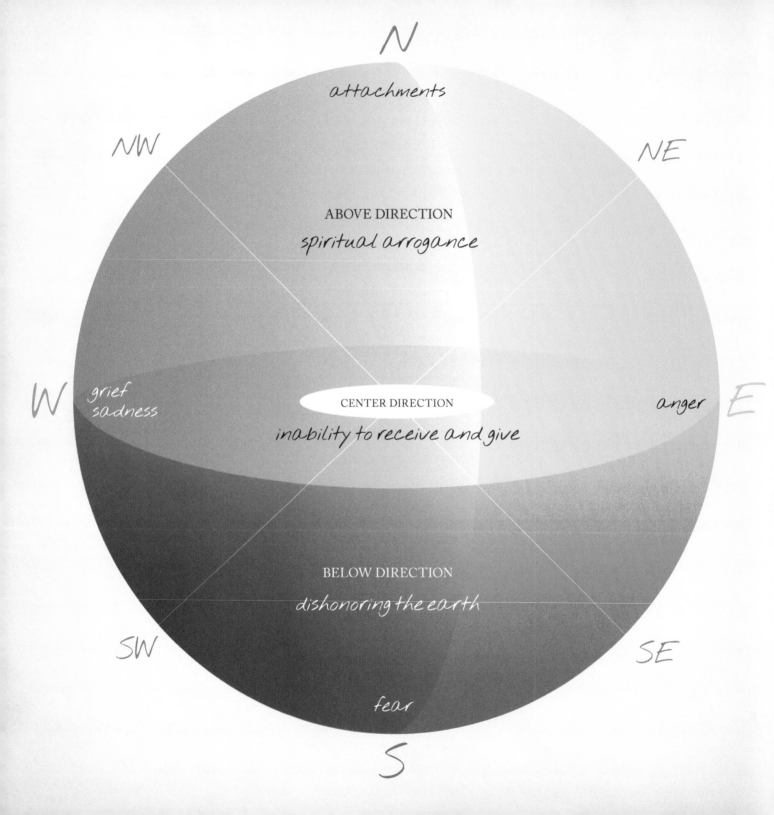

The Seven Causes of Illness

| SOUTHERN DIRECTION | The attribute of the South is *trust, love* and *innocence*. The cause of illness is *fear*. Negative projecting energies manipulate us by keeping us in a state of fear, anxiety, stress and apprehension. This energy causes contraction, defensiveness and mistrust. If you listen to the popular media in any country of the world, it is *fear* based and *fear* driven. The energy runs as a vibration affecting our entire central nervous system and our ability to be grounded. Look deeply within your internal landscape and name the fears you are carrying. *Fear* is a cause of illness that erodes self-confidence, self-reliance and self-awareness. It eats away the very ground of your being.

| WESTERN DIRECTION | The attributes of the West are *introspection, self-reflection* and *truth*. Truth gets distorted when emotions are not allowed space, time and the natural wave of expression. If contracted the human energy field develops into behavioral patterns of depression, victimization, un-expressed grief and there is a withdrawal from the organic process of soul development – a withdrawal from life. For example: It is estimated that 75% of the American population is on a mood altering prescribed drug. (Exception given for the physiological chemical need to balance the brain). This high percentage does not take into account the issues of alcohol abuse, recreational drugs, or hard-core illegal drugs. So here is the question. Why is our need to numb out so enormous? We are avoiding the powerful emotions of sadness and grief. This causes soul loss. My first book *Remembering The Ancestral Soul: Soul Loss and Recovery* (www.author house.com) explores the epidemic theme of soul loss and provides healing ways. Un-expressed sadness and grief is the cause of illness in the watery world of the West.

| NORTHERN DIRECTION | The attributes of the North are *discernment, wisdom, serenity* and *an open mind*. When the mind is not open judgment and attachment to outcomes enters in. *Attachments* to how it *should be* or, "a black or white outcome" world-view happens. Manipulation and control keeps us locked into old patterns and out dated beliefs that are generated from the ego-mind. A closed mind is a mind full of garbage. The mind recycles past experiences obsessively, never breaking out of the cycle into the present. We become possessed by our attachments.

| EASTERN DIRECTION | The attributes of the East are *faith, illumination, creativity* and *visions*. The energy that holds back our creative potential is *anger*. Anger directed inwardly or outwardly creates war. War is a state of self-destruction and chaos that cuts off our life force. It keeps us in a constant state of being off balance. Anger is fed by judgment and a lack of self-responsibility. Anger as a cause of illness effects how we relate with the physical world, emotional world, mental world and spiritual world.

| ABOVE DIRECTION | The attributes of the Above Directions are Star Ancestors, Father Sky, Father Sun and Mother Moon, our planetary cousins, *cosmic connection, universal wisdom, universal mind, unity consciousness*. The cause of illness is *spiritual arrogance*. The spiritual path is a tricky path. As soon as the ego talks you into the belief that you have become 'ego-less' spiritual arrogance comes in and possesses the individual. Anyone who skips over being human and moves into the "I'm above it all" is in a spiritual split. Spiritual arrogance is also known as "the bright shadow".

| BELOW DIRECTION | The attributes of the Below Direction are the *Devic Kingdoms*, the *Elementals Beings* of Mother Earth, *Mother Earth's Intelligence and Wisdom*, the *Subterraneans*. The cause of illness is *dishonoring and disrespect of earth*, and *her sentient beings and resources*. The roots of connection have been disconnected. The illness is a splitting from knowing that we are inter-related, what effects one being effects us all. *Dishonor and disrespect* is the cause of illness in the below direction.

| CENTER DIRECTION | The attribute is *now*. Present moment, only moment awareness. The ability to live in *balance*, with the attributes of *inclusivity, cooperation* and *community*. When the Center Direction is out of balance, there is an inability to receive and to give. The heart center is closed. Where there is selfishness a vortex in the center spins counter clockwise throwing off leaky energy. Expressed as narcissism, *all about me* presents as spiritual poverty. The illness is the *inability to receive and to give* in balance.

ATTRIBUTES AND LESSONS TO DISCOVER IN WORKING
WITH THE MEDICINE WHEEL

As we continue to traverse the Medicine Wheel, each phase or cycle of your life will arise. Here are some questions to support the development and growth of your soul. Feel free to insert your own questions in each section. Use the Medicine Wheel as a mirror.

| SOUTH EAST | Spirituality of the child self in balance with the rebirthing self. Perceiving the nature of realities. New beginnings and letting go of old outdated behaviors.

QUESTION – Can I envision my future? How? In what way can I bring forth my creativity? How may I work with the sum total of all of me in order to live a good life?

| SOUTH | Trust, love, innocence. Celebration of Life. Uncovering the past childhood experiences, shedding old skins of outmoded behaviors. Growth, individuation.

QUESTION – Review childhood and childhood wounding. Ask yourself in what manner do I need to become free in order to grow? Put down old stories that no longer serve you in order to move forward.

| SOUTH WEST | Place of change and initiation. Moving from a child-consciousness into another phase of life.

Moving towards introspection of the West – the shadow of what has not yet become uncovered.

QUESTION – What do I need in order to grow?

Teenage years; sexuality, rites of passage as you grow up. How can I honor my teen years in order to shed light upon the present?

QUESTION – What are my fears about discovering all of who I am?

| WEST | Unveiling illusions. Going inward to find deeper insights. Surrendering the *False Self/* Mask in the archaeological dig for the *True Self.* Finding inner authority, the spiritual adult. The Masks begin to be uncovered, how we have identified self in the world. Begin to understand the *trance-states* we have enacted to keep us hypnotized, recycling old patterns. The more subtle underlying messages begin to emerge.

Looking at areas in your life in which you are living from a dis-empowered state of being. Accepting that we have dark places inside. Unveiling secrets. Accepting your self now.

QUESTION – What truth do I need to discover so that I can shift the state of disempowerment and become fully responsible?

| NORTH WEST | Moving into ownership of personal power. Recognizing self, deepening intimacy and relationships with others. Understanding internal values and truths. A sense of inner justice develops. Accepting inner authority. Stepping into confidence and competency.

QUESTION – How am I avoiding or not showing up in relationship(s)? What are my fears of intimacy?

QUESTION – Where am I not fully confident? How can I be consistent in my life?

| NORTH | Wisdom, clarity of mind, serenity, intentionality (good will), strength, self-reflection.

Listening. Maturation cycle. The ability to discern develops. Discriminate with discernment versus judgment and intolerance.

Self-awareness and self-consciousness merges with strength of will (intentionality vs. willfulness).

QUESTION – Am I embodying all my life experience and able to share it with others?

QUESTION – Where am I forcing/pushing my will? (Look at willfulness vs. willingness.)

| NORTH EAST | The birth of the wise mind tempered by life experience. Walking your talk, designs of energy change, visions and self-empowerment.

Bringing mind to the illumination of thoughts and experiences of life. A movement towards the light of consciousness.

QUESTION – Is my mind clear and in good relationship with what I am experiencing? What changes are being presented?

QUESTION – Where am I seeking consciousness? How am I honoring my spiritual practices?

| EAST | Passion, creativity, illumination, action, playfulness, rebirth, enlightenment. Fire of the heart; all karmic knowledge is assimilated in the fire of purity.

QUESTION – Where are passion and creativity activated in my life? What do I need to manifest in my life now?

| SOUTH EAST | Flexibility and purpose in re-birthing into a new paradigm.

Change Cycle: Transformation/Transmutation

QUESTION – Are there areas in my life where I am burning out? How am I in right relationship with myself and all life?

5

THE MEDICINE WHEEL OF LIFE
the 9 Rs : a meditation to unwind trauma and stress

This meditation addresses
post and current traumatic stress dissonance,
as well as the more normal stress reactions
we experience day to day.

When I look at the insight questions in the previous section Attributes and Lessons I am reminded of a meditation I developed through the years of working with the Medicine Wheel as a vessel for self-healing. I developed this as a skillful tool for self-awareness, to bring me out of a trance state (like PTSD, Post Traumatic Stress Dissonance – which I call Dissonance rather than a Disorder relating to soul loss). Over years of private practice I have worked with Veterans, rape 'thrivers' vs. survivors; patients with physical, mental, emotional and spiritual abuse; families and individuals processing grief and suicide and end of life passage with patients. This healing meditation navigates the Medicine Wheel of Life. It unwinds stress reaction, step-by-step and breath-by-breath, bringing consciousness to discomfort, allowing it to be exactly what it is, acknowledging the life experience, feeling the wave and moving it forward with insight and stability. Post Traumatic Stress Dissonance (PTSD) is a major factor affecting almost every culture. The current traumatic stress dissonance not being addressed creates an energy field that feeds fear (one of the major causes of illness in the time we are living).

We begin in the South Eastern Direction; the home of change. The Graphic Chart shows the entry point of the 9 Rs beginning in the South East, circumnavigating the Medicine Wheel and coming into balance in the Center.

The awakening process is activated in us in one of two ways, as a challenge or as an ally. Our senses are activated and mobilized through our sensate body wisdom. When we invite our true feelings and own our body awareness, our blueprint comes forth for conscious activation and transformation.

The body holds memories from this life and from our past lives and our life between lives. Our 'blueprint' presents as life lessons. Each being on the journey to consciousness is contributing not only to awakening individually but also to the global collective consciousness awakening.

MEDITATION TO UNWIND TRAUMA AND STRESS

To be read to out loud as you traverse the Medicine Wheel. Preparation for each of the 9 Rs introduces the practice direction by direction. Begin this practice by choosing a life experience that activates you in a stressful way or which activates an old pattern.

|1 SOUTH EAST | Begin with four deep breathes and place yourself in the present moment in the South East of the Medicine Wheel. Breathe in through the nose and out through the mouth. Deep cleansing breathes. Say out loud, "I have just been activated by something that relates to a person, place or event, either past or present. I choose to awaken to this activation because I feel extreme discomfort and may not understand what is happening".

(Make a conscious commitment to yourself in this moment to breathe. As you breathe, allow yourself the space, place and time to *Relax* around your discomfort. Just let it be. Notice and observe.) *Breathe*. Relax your shoulders.

|2 SOUTH | As you continue breathing, take four deep breathes in through the nose and out through your mouth. Do not feel pressured by the outer world to give answers, or make decisions. Observe yourself breathing and notice how your body feels. *Rest* in the knowledge you are taking space for something else to arise. This is the practice of non-doing in the midst of

REMEMBER

Bringing conscious awareness in an awakened state into a gathering of self (soul retrieval). Coherency, calling together all aspects of self from past into present. Re-membering on cellular "soulular" levels.

RECOGNIZE

Recogniition of self that comes from understanding past and present. Person, Place, Thing Experience (PPTE) Timeline in life to present. Recognizing events that need healing and attention.

RECALIBRATE

Acknowledging your gifts and service (life task). Recalibrating life task at a different phase of life. Old patterns dissolve, a remembered/ coherent soul takes presidence. Integration

REFLECTION

Looking inward, allow deeper insights to come to the surface. Consciousnesss awakens. WIE model, shadow arises and is met without judgement.

RECEIVE

Integrate life lesson Receive the gifts and insight it brings. Balance and harmony.

RESPOND

"I am connected to the abundance of the universe" becomes real/ manifested and activated. Conscious language replaces old belief systems with new awakened being.

REJUVENATE

Self-nurturance; recharging on all levels of energy. A deeper commitment to wellness and taking steps to implement them. Exercise meditation, spiritual practices on a daily basis.

REST

Letting go of stress, tension by getting rest, silence, quiet time. The practice is non-doing. Creating time and space daily for silence, enough sleep; energy begins to open up.

RELAX

Waking up inside discomfort. Recognizing overwhelm, anxiety, exhaustion, overdoing. Making a conscious commitment to change the pattern. Disengaging and unwinding from old patterns. Bring breathe to discomfort.

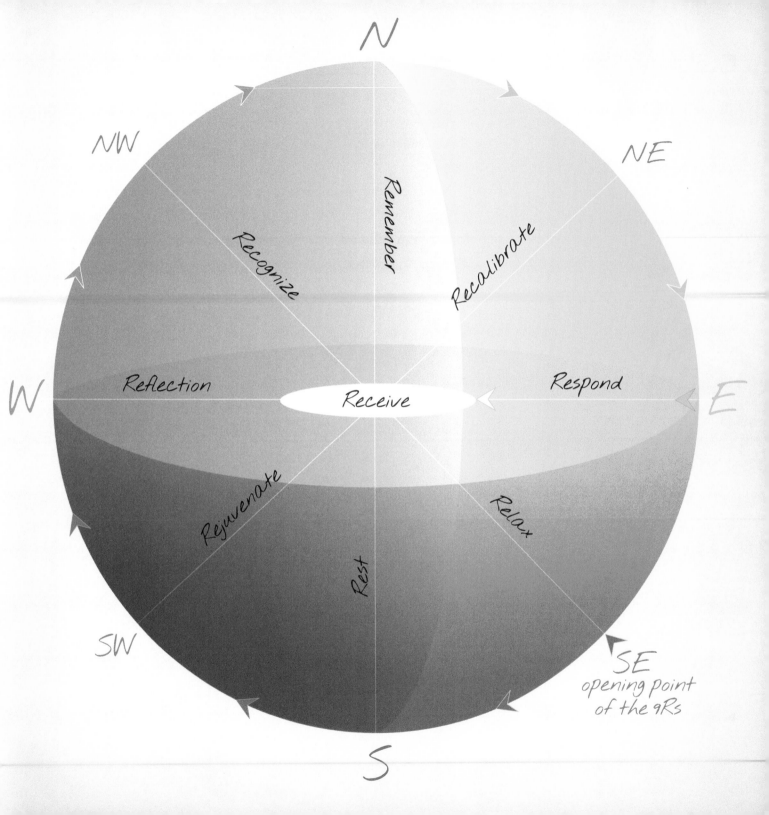

N

NW   NE

Remember

Recognize   Recalibrate

W   Reflection   Receive   Respond   E

Rejuvenate   Relax

Rest

SW   SE

SE
opening point
of the 9Rs

S

chaos. Allow your heart to expand in these moments. Say out loud, " I am creating space in my body to open into the deeper wisdom of my human energy field – which is a vast space of wisdom". *Breathe*.

|3 SOUTH WEST| As you continue to take the inward breath through your nose and outward breath through your mouth allow your self non-reactive space. You will notice that your energy is being *Rejuvenated*. You are not leaking your energy or being over responsible to make another feel comfortable, or to make a decision. Say out loud, "I am holding my energy field and staying contained within it. I am "holding my own". This is a huge step in self-awareness. *Breathe*.

|4 WEST| Continuing to breathe deepens self-awareness and the emotions that come with it. In the West, you move with your breath into self-reflection. Breathe four times in through nose and out through your mouth, letting go each time. You allow all that is asking to come forward in your sensate energy field to arise. Breath through what is being presented. Understanding, insight and *Reflection* comes as you breathe each breath. Take three steps back and observe yourself as you experience what is being presented. *Breathe*. Say out loud, "I am the witness".

|5 NORTH WEST| As you are able to witness yourself you gain a sense of a time-line as to what was "then" and what is "now". *Recognizing* what needs your attention for healing in the present moment. Say out loud, "What is in the past needs reconciliation. As I continue to breathe and create internal space, I create a place within my self for healing".

|6 NORTH | Breathing into your mind allows more awareness. Say out loud, "I choose to remember and to connect to the life lessons I have come here to learn and to heal in this life time." *Remember*ing is connecting with your soul's blueprint. Your *soulular* memory is your cellular memory. They are the same thing. *Breathe.*

|7 NORTH EAST | As you allow yourself to acknowledge the past, you also see your gifts. Your gifts provide creative energy for a shift to take place. Breathe in through the nose and out through the mouth, four times. In the North Eastern direction, you experience *Re-calibration* as you connect to the *coherent* gifted soul that is you. Say out loud," I recognize, accept and understand my life lesson in this moment. I freely, clearly and completely send any negative cords of connection that do not belong to me back to the source from which they come. Through that source, I send back all negative cords that do not belong to me to the Great Central Sun to be dissolved. I am free." Say this out loud as many times as your need as you clear your energy field from negative attachments. *Breathe.*

|8 EAST | As you unwind cords from the past and recalibrate, another energy arises. It is as the energy of the universe beckoning you forward like a child full of wonder calling you to the next place of your awareness. In the Eastern gate the energy is to *Respond* (vs. react). Say out loud, "I am connected to the abundance of the universe and I choose to manifest_____, NOW!" (You fill in the blank with what you are visualizing as a positive outcome for yourself.) *Breathe.*

| 9 CENTER OF THE WHEEL | Visualize yourself moving in a state of grace and excitement into the balanced place at the very center of the Medicine Wheel. This is the place where you *Receive* insight. You have cleared a life lesson by activating positive will to transform. Say out loud, "I understand and accept myself completely, fully and with love. I am balanced and in harmony with myself and all life."

When you become reactionary again in the future, begin the process of moving around the Medicine Wheel until you come full circle back into balance and harmony in the center. *Breathe.*

6

THE FOUR BIG MOON CYCLES OF LIFE
and the medicine wheel

How to use the Big Moon Cycles
to track significant events
and times in your life

INTRODUCTION

Our physical, emotional, mental and spiritual bodies undergo a change in biorhythm every 9 months. Gestation is 9 months from conception to birth; developmental stages of growth continue in 9 month cycles throughout our lives. Nine-month cycles complete the directions in the medicine wheel in circles of nine (see diagram #1; The Big South Moon: ages 0-27+ years has 9 smaller wheels within the larger wheel that calibrate biorhythmic change every 9 months). Each Big Moon Cycle is close to what is known in astrology as a *Saturn Return*. A *Saturn Return* is a time of recalibration, reassessing life goals and life lessons. Often it is a time of deep transformation and change after having traversed the Medicine Wheel one full cycle.

The Big Moon Cycles were introduced to me by Roshi Joan Halifax from the work of her Cherokee teacher, Hyemeyohsts Storm as a form of referencing life events in a context that provide deeper meaning. The ancient teachings are from indigenous star knowledge. The number 9 represents completion and transformation – a coming out of the chrysalis in a new form.

I include the charts of the Big Moon Cycles here as a tool for tracking significant events and times in your life. Also as a means to open your inner awareness to the biorhythms connecting the dots of your life cycles. Keep in mind that this is approximate (each person has a unique biorhythm). Each of us works with particular life lessons, in the timing that is most appropriate. It is insightful to go back into the charts to track certain important events in life and to see when they occurred. The stage or phase of life, the direction and its meaning become apparent when you look at the charts. I feel the Big Moon Cycles provide a road map that helps us become more aware of the journey we have traversed. It supports us more in understanding the ground and consciousness upon which we stand in the present moment. The charts provide deeper meaning to life lessons. In reviewing the cycles and time you gain insights into your past. More awareness comes forth as you *remember* yourself with more clarity. Some life lessons begin to stand out in sharp relief as you allow yourself to reflect upon the past. The emphasis is on reflection and insight, not reattaching to an old story. You can also see themes in your present life.

Make time to be with a specific place on the wheel that calls to you in the first 27 years of your life cycle. Look back and remember what was happening during this time period. Practice "reviewing the movie" as though it were someone else's life and you are witnessing it in a state of open-heart and relaxed attention. Create a time line of certain events in your life that have meaning. Draw a large circle on a piece of blank paper. Search back into your personal history about friends, moving, schools, teachers, places, family, significant events and memories that come up for you as you review the first 27 years of your life. Journal these and allow awareness to arise using the Witness, Inquirer, Experiencer model. Go back to the Medicine Wheel as described, look at the time lines in the first 27 years and begin to make dots on the wheel or inside the wheel that depict certain crucial or important moments you recall. Use the circle and the time line as a creative way to see your life as a round vessel contained in an ancient form of protection and wholeness. Journal. Ask your dreams to inform you about these moments, these life experiences. Particularly, look at the Cardinal Directions and the years in each Big Moon Cycle that they embody. Look back at your life during these years and reflect upon what was happening. Then look at the Semi-Cardinal Directions, which are between each major Cardinal point of South, West, North and East. Look at South East, South West, North West, North East as initiation points or times of shift and change.

As an example 60.9 year in the Big North Moon is in the South of the small inner wheel, placed directly in the South of the large Medicine Wheel. Look at what is written in the South as the present energy. The Semi-Cardinal Direction of the South East represents where you have just come from, in this case a *Saturn Return* which is a time of recalibration and the beginning of eldership. The South West represents how you will be shifting and adjusting as you traverse inside the wheel within the wheel from age 60.9 to age 63. The challenging energy across the wheel that you are learning about is understanding how to use your discernment as a mentor and peacemaker.

In your dreaming/visioning/or meditation practice ask: What does my soul need in order to grow?

Listen to the dreams and reflections. Write down the messages from your soul.

How is your soul asking you to grow in consciousness? What are your gifts? What are some of the life lessons you have chosen to learn and clear this lifetime?

Every step of the way we have help, we have support, we have mentors, teachers and guidance in this world and in the spiritual worlds. Every moment is a healing moment. One of the greatest forms of help is self-awareness – coming to self-consciousness. The Medicine Wheel supports us in looking at phases, cycles and stages of awareness. The Wheel holds a mirror so that we can recognize an opportunity to heal from our past, thus becoming free and present.

Working with the Medicine Wheel of Life reveals opportunities for personal transformation. It is through observing ourselves and our behavior that allows the spiritual adult to come forth. Freeing the senses brings forth the potential to live differently. You can grow out of living in a defensive Mask. Uncovering the *trance-state* underneath the Mask is the core awareness our soul is striving to bring to consciousness. When you identify the core, a greater part of you is unleashed. You move beyond the past. Power and life force is available to be used in creative, life affirming ways. This is our *True Self* – the galloping, joyful, playful manifesting being who is in total love with life, the planet and everything! To live this way is our birthright. It is also a right of passage. How each one of us finds our way in and through is part of the soul's unique mystery. Activating our senses within the vessel of the Medicine Wheel allows us to have a model upon which to grow and move forward.

In each successive wheel the cycle brings forth life lessons. Repeating life lessons and behaviors that have not been learned and freed will arise in the subsequent Big Moon Cycles. Tracking them and becoming aware of what is being shown through your life experience is a way to evolve your soul. Your soul's wisdom is available to you from past experience and phases of development in the Medicine Wheel.

The Medicine Wheel of Life helps us to open to questions relating to how we are living life. Using the wheel as a container incubates insights and awareness. At every moment we have free will and free choice to shift. We can move through recycling over and over again or choose to transform our behavior.

All beings have the potential to be fully realized at any moment. Some of us have forgotten who we have come here to be. We have the ability to remember ourselves every moment.

Balancing body, emotions, mind and spirit naturally brings forth transformation. Practice (or skillful means) produces profound shift in consciousness, strength and confidence. When you have a cellular experience of inner change, the body's wisdom really gets it! It gets very excited, releasing all sorts of wonderful happy hormones. The conscious commitment to grow the soul is a *biggy*. The soul's natural inclination is to evolve.

EXAMPLE: THE BIG SOUTH MOON (AGES 0-27)

The direction outlined relates to the first turning of the Medicine Wheel from inception, birth, infancy, childhood, early latency, latency, early teenage time through to late teens, early adulthood, to age 27 (the beginning of the first *Saturn Return*). The turn of the wheel is known as The Big South Moon Wheel relating to aspects of our lives in which we first identify "who we are". In the first turning of the wheel, life lessons are brought forward as opportunities for soul growth. For example we begin to understand when we are living from a state of *True Self* or when we are in a defensive state known as the Mask, *False-Self*. We also experience the subtler hypnotic *trance-states* in our early years. *Trance-states* are a form of self-soothing repeating energetic patterns in order to stay disengaged (and disempowered) from life experiences. We can use The Big South Moon to track these energies when they were first enacted. The first 27 years are the foundation of images, beliefs, defenses and behavioral patterns we identify as our wounded nature, conversely we also learn our gifts during the Big South

Moon. Underneath each Mask and *trance-state* is a truer form of who you are. Any time you find yourself going into a foggy, unclear state – it is a *trance-state* and there has been some form of soul loss during this developmental period. Masks are the first defense, *trance-states* are the secondary defense which represents some form of soul loss. We will work with both types of defenses with skillful means practices in the Mask chapters of the book.

The Big Moon Cycles of Life:
The Big South Moon: Ages 0-27 years
The Big West Moon: Ages 27-54 years
The Big North Moon: Ages 54-81 years
The Big East Moon: Ages 81-108 years

YOUNG ADULT

mental discernment

clarity of purpose

power

air

TEEN TO
EARLY ADULT

the unknown

mystery

justice

value systems

ADULT

approaching transition

clarity of vision

*shifting balance and
attitudes*

big south moon

TEENAGE

emotional truth

water

SPIRITUAL INCEPTION
AND BIRTH

space

ADULT

spiritual

faith

setting intention for next life cycle

initiation

fire

0-27 years

PUBERTY

place of initiations

curiosity

magic and dreams

transition

CHILDHOOD

physical

trust

growth

individuation

latency phase of development

and independence

earth

EARLY
CHILDHOOD

place of new beginnings

new discoveries

infancy/youth

to mid-childhood

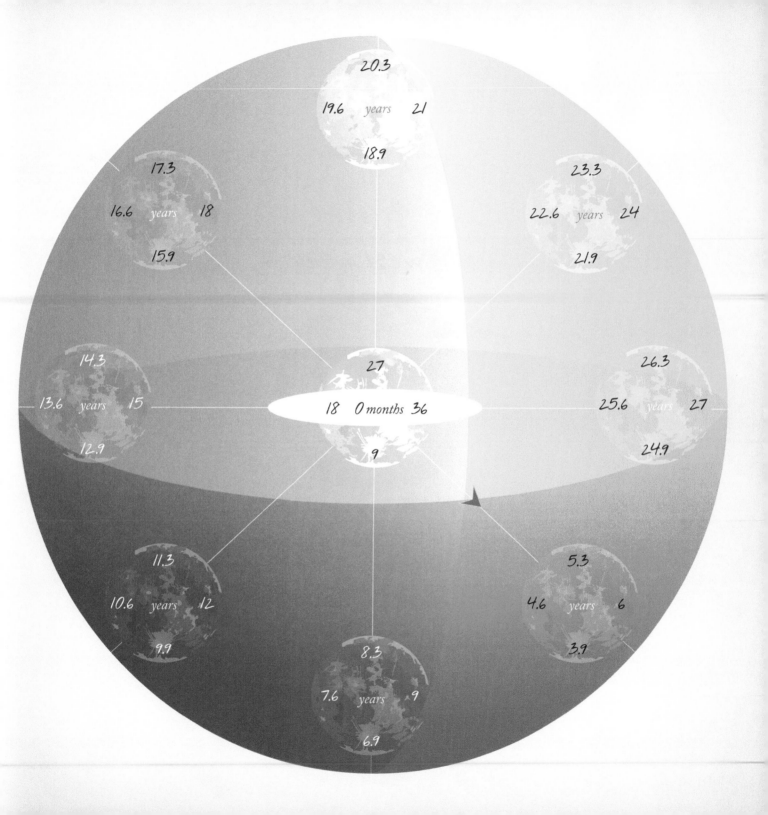

MENTAL DISCERNMENT
*deeper understanding
of personal values
and how they are lived*
air

*developing depth
of character*

*beginning
self-reflection of
life lessons repeating to
become springboard
for changes
in behavior*

big west moon

EMOTIONAL TRUTH
*becoming conscious of
personal power*
water

FIRST SATURN RETURN
recalibration cycle
space

SPRIRITUAL FAITH
*initiation
renegotiation of life purpose
and goals*
fire

27–54 years

*initiation
shifting into
more awareness of self
and behaviors*

*renewal or completion
of soul contract
first full cycle of
Medicine Wheel
entering a new cycle
of awareness*

PHYSICAL TRUST
*resetting goals
redefining self in world*
earth

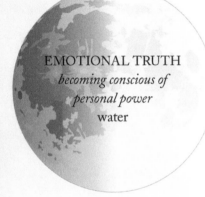

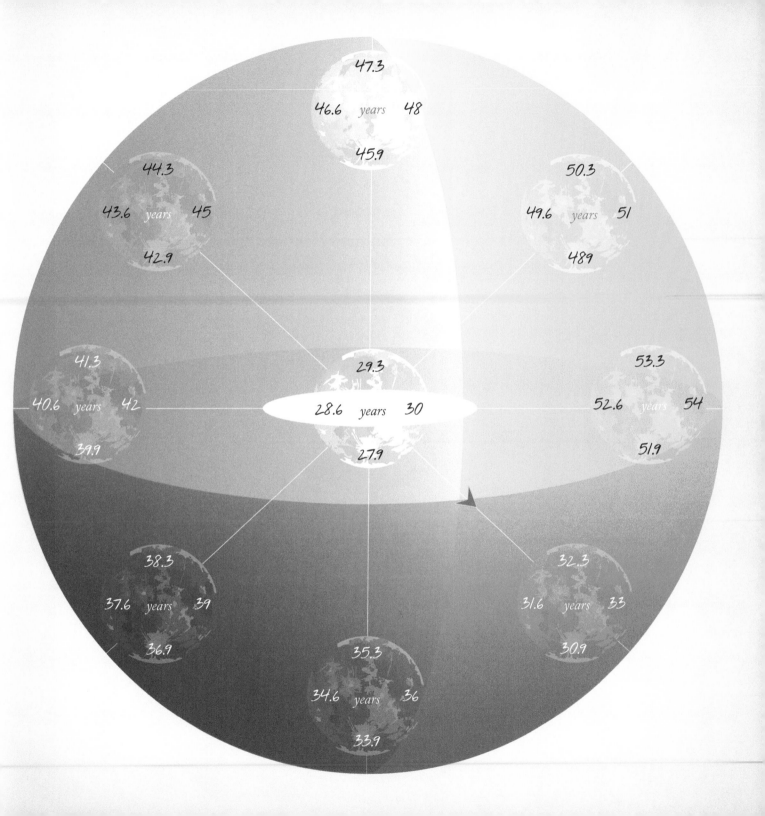

MENTAL DISCERNMENT

teaching/wisdon-keeper
universal understanding
power, peacemaker
serenity

air

value systems
shift
reflecting upon law of the
universe/cosmos

shifting balance and
attitudes
"talk your walk" cycle

big north moon

EMOTIONAL TRUTH

eldership
meditation cycle-insights
become more collective
in consciousness

water

SECOND SATURN RETURN

recalibration cycle
space

SPIRITUAL FAITH

inward spiritual cycle
self reflection
self acceptance
life review

fire

54-81 years

initiation
changes and shifting
toward more
inner balance

beginning eldership
menopause, "men-pause"
shift in personal identity

PHYSICAL TRUST

making other life choices
grounding into next phase
of becoming an elder

earth

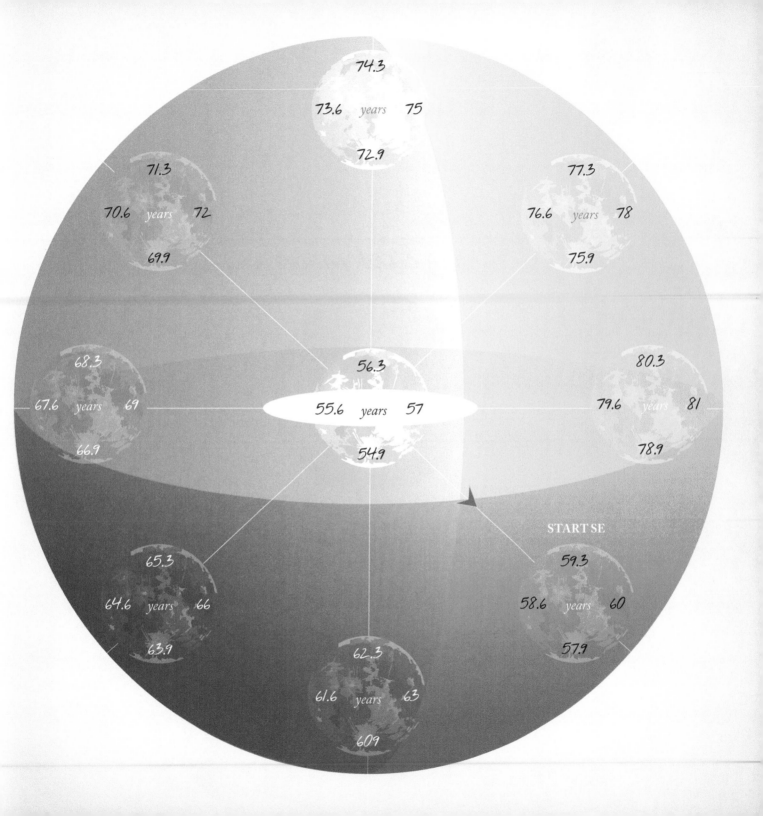

MENTAL DISCERNMENT
spiritual elder
wisdon-keeper
air

exploration of unknown

shifting perspectives

big east moon

EMOTIONAL TRUTH
vision turns inward
letting go of
physical outer world

THIRD SATURN RETURN
recalibration cycle
space

SPIRITUAL TREASURE
faith
fire

81–108 years

initiations
magic and dreams
letting go of the past

birth/ death
initiation
life review
exploring death

CHILDHOOD REVISITED
trust deepening on spiritual levels
putting down regrets
making peace
earth

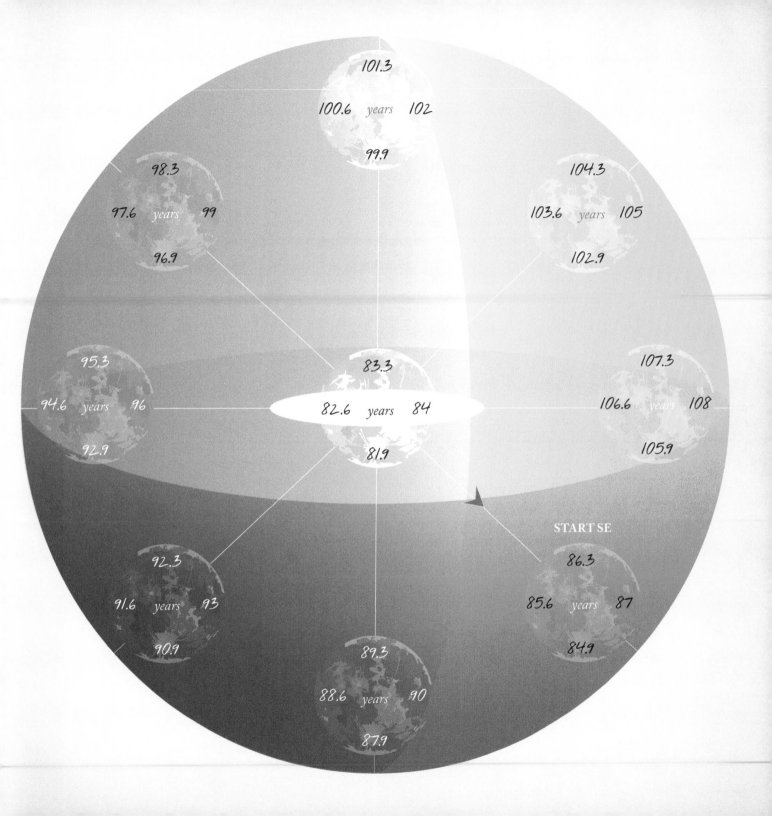

7

THE PHYSICAL MEDICINE WHEEL
creating the medicine wheel in nature

You can create your own Medicine Wheel
in your backyard and walk it daily,
do ceremony and prayers there.
Meditate and find balance in the vessel
of the Medicine Wheel.

THE STONES ARE AS FOLLOWS

CENTER STONE – Creator, all sentient life, unity
- all colors are represented in the tree of life
- all plants and animals, all life force

SECOND STONE – Earth Mother energy
- warmth and healing, nurturance, bonding, stability, growth
- colors are green, red, brown
- plants are squash, corn, beans, nutrition is cultivated

THIRD STONE – Father Sky, Father Sun energy, Star Nations – The Above Directions
- spirituality, ceremony, healing the soul, the psyche of wisdom
- color is sky blue
- plant is the sunflower; a good heart is cultivated

FOURTH STONE – Grandmother Moon energy
- magical properties, purity of spirit, balance
- color is silver
- plant is mugwort; dreaming is cultivated

FIFTH STONE – Plant Earth energy
- growth, stability, strength, courage, foundation, groundedness, gravity
- colors are all colors found in nature
- plants are all plants found upon the earth

SIXTH STONE – Wind and Air energies

- cleansing, purification, spiral energy
- color is clear or white
- plants are all airborne seeded ones such as milkweed, dandelions, etc.

SEVENTH STONE – Fire energies

- power, fearlessness, action, change, transformation
- colors are yellow and red
- plant is the fireweed

EIGHTH STONE – Water energies

- mystery, reflection, introspection, the thunder beings and the tides of change, waves of life
- color is deep indigo blue or black
- plant is the iris

The eight stones are placed in a circle in the center of the Medicine Wheel. Then Four Cardinal Directional stones are placed. A red stone in the South, a blue or black stone in the West, a white stone in the North and a yellow stone in the East. Smaller stones placed radiate from the central 8 in the circle outward like four equal spokes of a wheel to the Four Cardinal Directions. In between the Four Cardinal Directional Stones, you can place smaller stones that represent the passage of time and the seasons. Two stones placed equally between each Cardinal Directional Stone will fill out the Medicine Wheel, representing the months in the calendar year. *See diagram.*

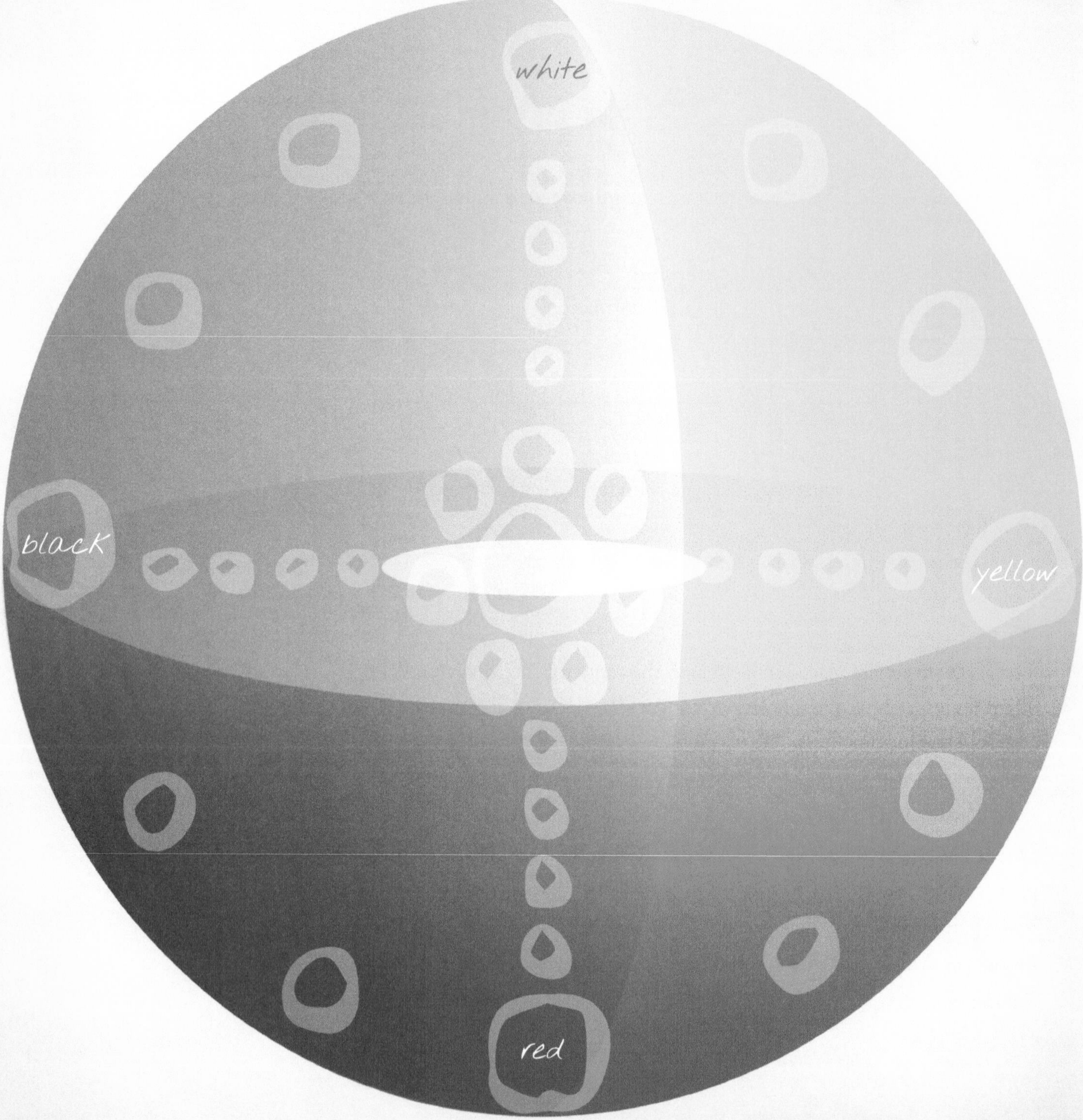
white
black
yellow
red

8 stones in Center
4 Cardinal Directions
2 stones between the Four Cardinal Directions
12 stones form the outer circle
representing 12 months of the year

the physical medicine wheel

| CRYSTALS AND STONE MEDICINE WHEEL ALTARS |

Crystals and Stones have been used
by indigenous cultures
for millennia
for energy medicine healing
and as catalytic
amplifiers for prayers.

Used as a grid, the altar balances, harmonizes and heals home, office, personal altar or global grid with which you are praying. When you set up your Stone and Crystal Altar make your intention very clear as to the purpose of the altar. See Melody's book: Love is in the Earth (updated reference), Earth Love Publishing House for information about preparing stones and crystals as energy medicine amplifiers. The following are some suggestions for setting-up a crystal and stone Medicine Wheel Altar. (If you refer back to the Seven Cardinal Directions, it will be helpful as you gather your stones and crystals and set your intention for the grid/altar).

| 1 | SOUTH EAST – New beginnings and change, moving from one phase of life into another (Semi-Cardinal transition point in the Medicine Wheel)

| ELEMENT | Fire to earth (Spirit incarnates into physical body)

| COLOR | Orange

| ENERGY MEDICINE | Change, transformation, birth, death

| STONES | Carnelian, Fire Agate, Tangerine Quartz, Orange Quartz, Creedite

| 2 | SOUTH
Grounding, trust

| ELEMENT | Earth

| COLOR | Red

| ENERGY MEDICINE | Trust, Love, Innocence

| CAUSE OF ILLNESS | Fear

| STONES | Red Jasper, Red Garnet, Quartz with Chlorite, Red Granite, Smokey Quartz

| 3 | SOUTH WEST
Place of Initiation, moving from one phase of life into another
(Semi-Cardinal transition point in the Medicine Wheel)

| ELEMENT | Earth to Water (especially subterranean waters)

| COLOR | Turquoise, Sky Blue

| ENERGY MEDICINE | Movement forward, Puberty, Exploration, Curiosity

| STONES | Turquoise, Aquamarine, Blue Quartz, Blue and Black Kyanite

| 4 | WEST

Place of Introspection; home of truth; the emotional body

| ELEMENT | Water

| COLOR | Black or deep midnight blue

| ENERGY MEDICINE | Emotional body; purification, inspiration, development of emotions

| CAUSE OF ILLNESS | Unexpressed grief and/or sadness.

| STONES | Tibetan Black Quartz, Black Tourmaline, Apache Tear, Jet, Obsidian

|5|NORTH WEST

Development of values and sense of justice. Also, awe, magic and wonder (transition point)

|ELEMENT| Water to Air

|COLOR| Green

|ENERGY MEDICINE| Inner world consciousness and life experiences are brought to the outer world; a change of pace and movement forward; looking at habits and behavioral patterns, what is working/what patterns are not working

|STONES| Oceanic Jasper, Verde Quartz, Ponamu (New Zealand Jade), Green Apophyllite, Green Jade, Chlorite Septer, Green Phantom Quartz, Seraphanite

|6|NORTH
Discernment. Intellectual Mind and Heart Mind

|ELEMENT| Air

|COLOR| White

|ENERGY MEDICINE| The development of discernment (vs. judgment). Insightful thinking.

|CAUSE OF ILLNESS| Attachments (to ego, agendas, control, judging self and others)

|STONES| Clear White Quartz, White Selenite, White Turquoise

|7|NORTH EAST
Place of dreams, visions, future (transitional energy)

|ELEMENT| Air to Fire

|COLOR| Lavender, violet

|ENERGY MEDICINE| Visions and dreams for the future; a movement and change cycle in the Medicine Wheel

|STONES| Amethyst, Tanzanite, Lavender Quartz, Alexandrite, Ajoite

Illumination, spiritual faith, creativity, transmutation

|E L E M E N T | Fire

|C O L O R | Yellow

|E N E R G Y   M E D I C I N E | Far sighted vision, creativity, passion, alchemy
to shift from the material world to spiritualizing matter and being in the
spiritual realms

|C A U S E   O F   I L L N E S S | Anger (rage, jealousy, hate)

|S T O N E S | Sunstone Crystal, Sulphur, Citrine Crystal, Fire Opal,
Yellow Quartz

|9|CENTER, ABOVE AND BELOW DIRECTION

All That Is. *Center* is Balance and harmony. *Above Direction* is Celestial Beings and Star Nations. *Below Direction* is Devic Kingdom and the Subterranean Beings.

|ELEMENT| All – earth, water, air, fire and space (*The Great Mystery That Moves Through All Things* is the essence of space)

|COLOR| All colors

|ENERGY MEDICINE| Balance is both receiving and giving; the Sacred Human Heart is open, receptive and aware

|CAUSE OF ILLNESS| Spiritual arrogance, greed, power-over/ control and manipulation

|STONES| Rose Quartz, Devic Kingdom Quartz, Spirit Quartz Amethyst or Citrine, Super Seven Stone, Red Feldspar, Angelite Anhydrite; Diamond, Zircon, White Sapphire, Preseli Blue Stone

North:
Clear Quartz Orb

North West:
Green Apophyllite

North East:
Spirit Wand Amethyst

West:
Apache Tear
Obsidian

Center:
Dog Tooth Quartz Heart

East:
Citrine Quartz

South West: Turquoise

South East: Creedite

South: Red Jasper

the physical medicine wheel

| THE HUMAN ENERGY FIELD AND THE MEDICINE WHEEL |

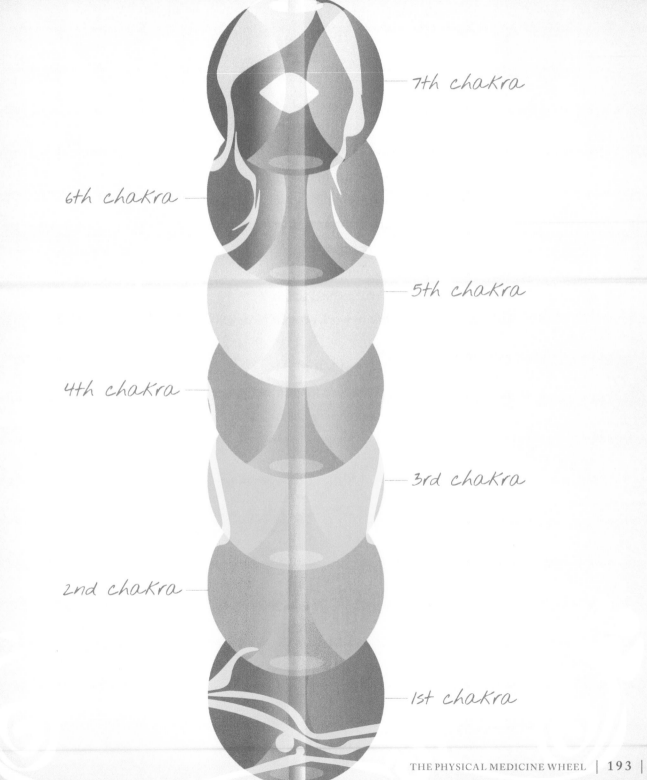

7th chakra

6th chakra

5th chakra

4th chakra

3rd chakra

2nd chakra

1st chakra

CHAKRAS 1-3 REPRESENT OUR CONNECTION
TO THE PHYSICAL WORLD

|3RD CHAKRA|

- Who you are in the world – self image
- How you connect to self and to others
- Intention towards others
- Intuitive center
- Self healing intentionality
- Your will to heal self
- Ability to work on self; to develop and evolve

Chakras 1-3

|2ND CHAKRA|

- Quality of love for self and partner
- Pleasure receiver
- Quantity of sexual energy
- The power pack – pleasure sender

|1ST CHAKRA|

- Physical energy connects to the planet and the whole
- *Lifeforce Pump* "I am here now."
- Grounded to earth, grounded into physical world

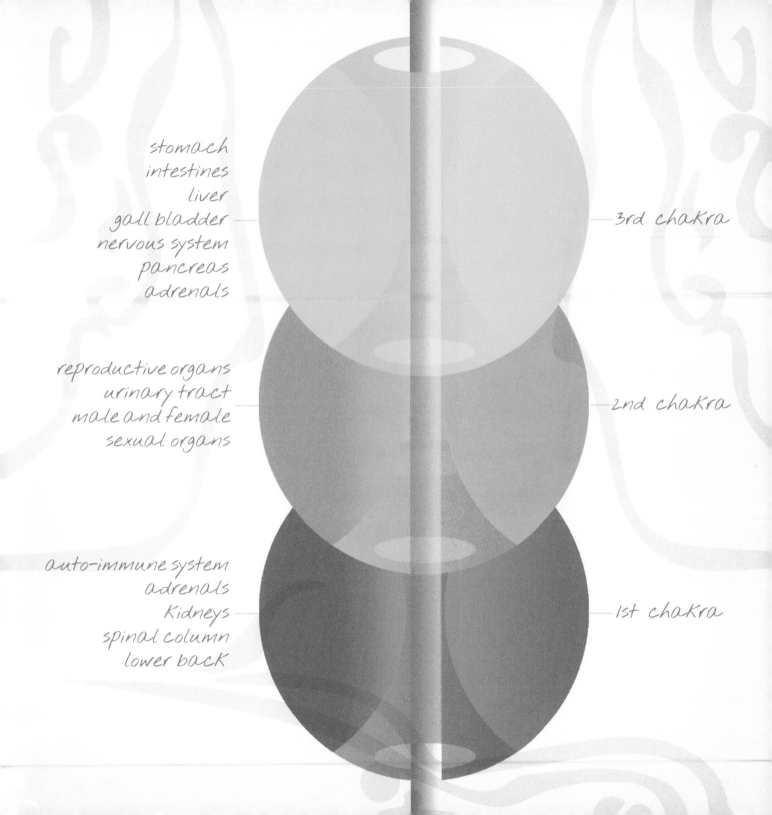

stomach
intestines
liver
gall bladder
nervous system
pancreas
adrenals

3rd chakra

reproductive organs
urinary tract
male and female
sexual organs

2nd chakra

auto-immune system
adrenals
Kidneys
spinal column
lower back

1st chakra

4th chakra —

breasts
lungs
thymus
heart, blood flow
vagus nerve
circulation
upper shoulders

CHAKRA 4 IS THE BRIDGE BETWEEN THE PHYSICAL WORLD,
THE EMOTIONAL WORLD AND THE SPIRITUAL WORLD

| 4TH CHAKRA |
- The bridge between the physical and spiritual worlds through the sacred
  human heart
- Love for humanity and all sentient beings
- Compassion for self and others
- Ego, how will is used in the outer world
- Willingness vs. willfulness
- Attachments

Chakra 4

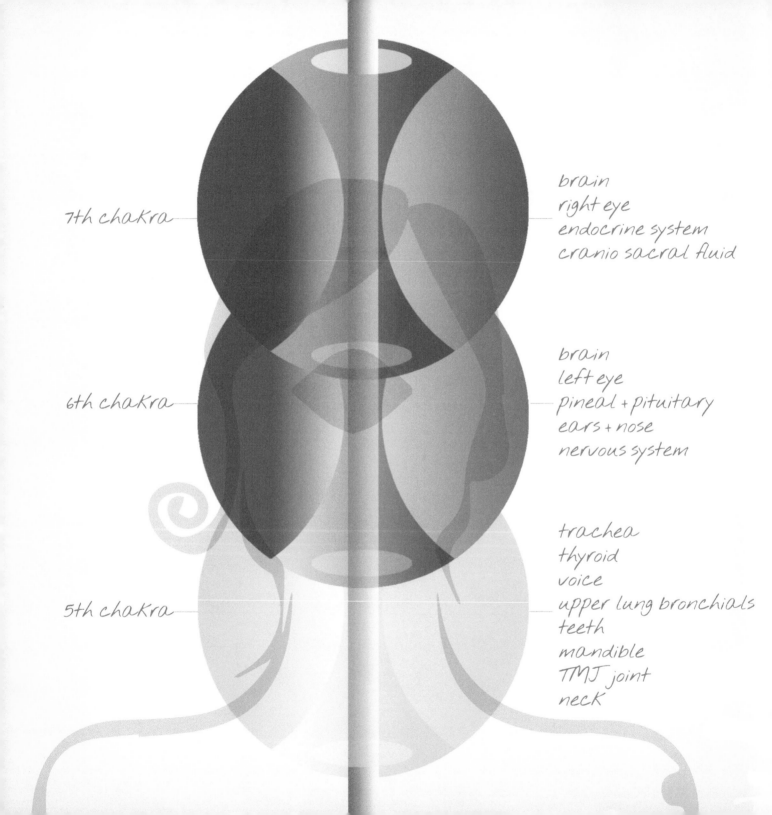

7th chakra

brain
right eye
endocrine system
cranio sacral fluid

6th chakra

brain
left eye
pineal + pituitary
ears + nose
nervous system

5th chakra

trachea
thyroid
voice
upper lung bronchials
teeth
mandible
TMJ joint
neck

CHAKRAS 5-7 REPRESENT THE MENTAL WORLD
TO THE SPIRITUAL WORLD

|7TH CHAKRA|

- Spiritual connections and integration
- Unity consciousness
- Connected with Star Ancestors and cosmic intelligence
- Able to access "knowing" transmission from spiritual connections
- Choice to incarnate into physical world

|6TH CHAKRA|

- Visualize and understand mental concepts
- Intuitive and intellectual path to psychic abilities, telepathy
- Ability to carry out ideas and concepts = mental executive
- Senses and sees on psychic levels: processes senses into physical reality

Chakra 5-7

|5 TH CHAKRA|

- Bridge to spiritual will unfolding
- Self responsibility
- Taking-in and assimilating; communication; sending and receiving
- Being heard through voice
- Sense of self within society
- Professional center; career satisfaction
- Intention toward self and others

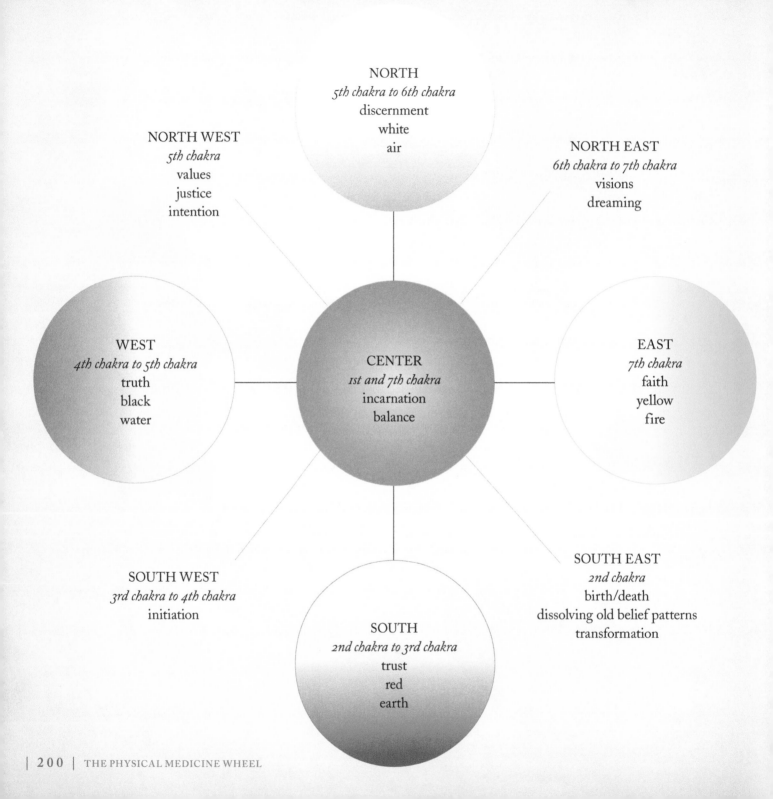

NORTH
5th chakra to 6th chakra
discernment
white
air

NORTH WEST
5th chakra
values
justice
intention

NORTH EAST
6th chakra to 7th chakra
visions
dreaming

WEST
4th chakra to 5th chakra
truth
black
water

CENTER
1st and 7th chakra
incarnation
balance

EAST
7th chakra
faith
yellow
fire

SOUTH WEST
3rd chakra to 4th chakra
initiation

SOUTH EAST
2nd chakra
birth/death
dissolving old belief patterns
transformation

SOUTH
2nd chakra to 3rd chakra
trust
red
earth

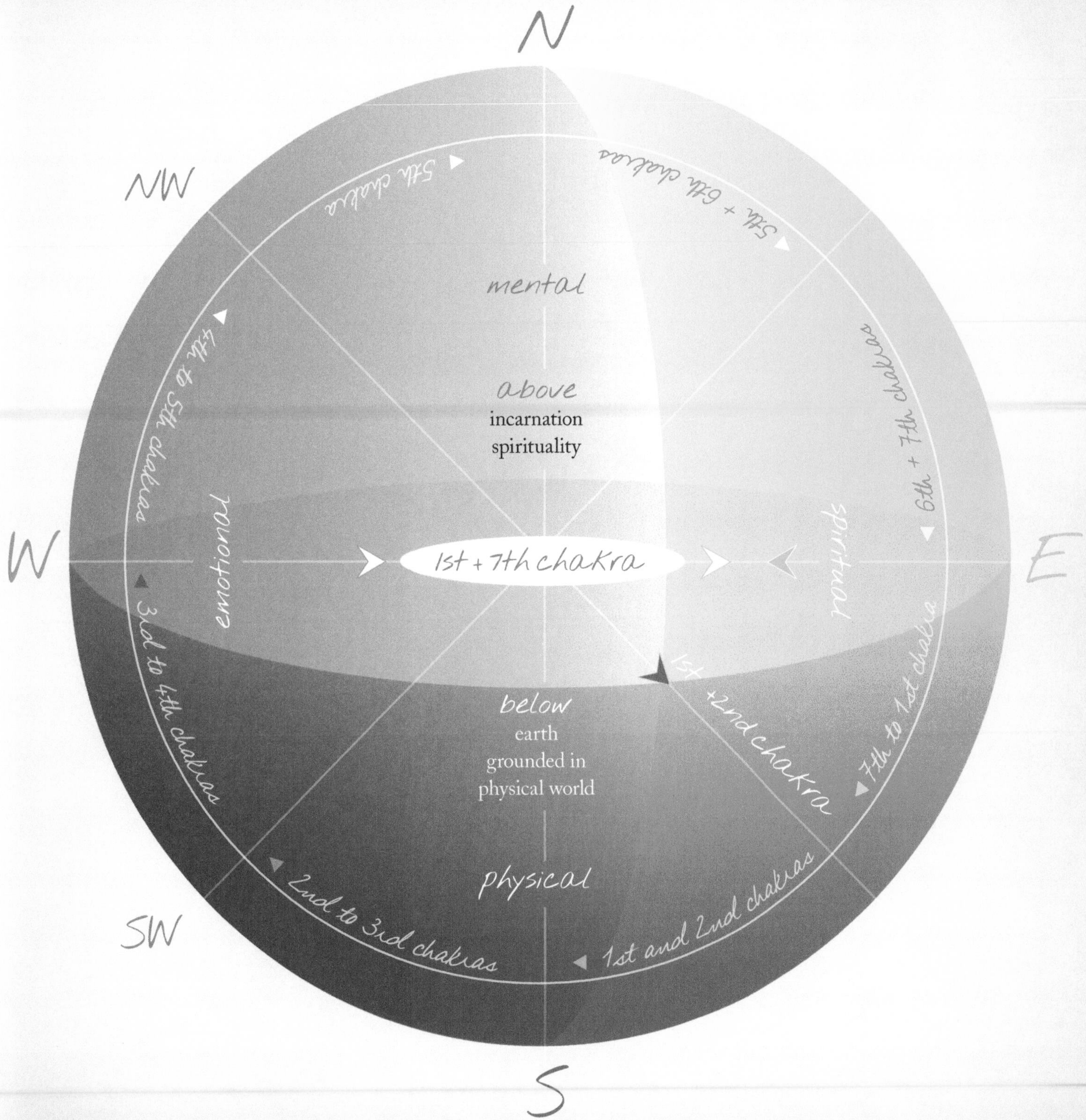
N
NW
W
E
SW
S
5th chakra
5th + 6th chakras
mental
4th to 5th chakras
6th + 7th chakras
above
incarnation
spirituality
emotional
spiritual
1st + 7th chakra
3rd to 4th chakras
7th to 1st chakras
1st +2nd chakra
below
earth
grounded in
physical world
physical
2nd to 3rd chakras
1st and 2nd chakras

8

MASKS

*introduction to the masks:
becoming conscious and staying conscious*

The mask is an energy form
that keeps us from our *True Self.*
It is actually an illusion
but when we attach our identity to it,
it becomes an energy form
that we relate to as being who we are.
The Mask is a form of ego-identification,
or a self-induced entity
that actually can possess our mind.

"To end the misery that has afflicted the human condition for thousands of years, you have to start with yourself and take responsibility for your inner state at any given moment. That means now." (*A New Earth*, Eckhart Tolle) When one or more of the Causes of Illness is experienced, we have a choice to defend with our Mask or to shift. The Seven Causes of Illness are Fear, Grief, Attachments, Anger, Disconnection from Earth and the Devic Kingdoms, Spiritual Arrogance and a Closed Heart; Inability to Receive and Give in Balance. These are dense forms of very powerful energies. When we are activated by the Seven Causes of Illness we cover over these energies with a "shell" or a Mask. The effect of this is that we stifle a part of our *True Self* by going into hiding behind the Mask. The Mask can also be a blatant form of denial or a defensive energy put in place to block and resist change.

Some of the characteristics of the Mask when activated are the following (these are only a few creative behaviors in our big bag of tricky Masks):

| IN-AUTHENTICITY | The False Face Mask. "Everything is fine." Or "I'm above it all."

| SUBMISSION | Collapse under pressure, rolling over under the wave of the "power-over" energy. Helpless and hopeless Mask.

| DEFENSIVENESS | Rigid behavior, brittleness, pushing back with anger or righteous indignation.

| PERFECTIONISM | The idealized self is rigid with appropriate behavior, being right is an imperative message of this Mask. Right and Uptight.

| NUMBNESS | Withdrawal, silent brooding, little to no contact with outer world, separation from self and others, isolation.

| SELF-JUSTIFICATION | Know it all, judging others, arrogant in relationships, uses the "power-over" energy to make others submit.

| DENIAL | Disconnected/split from feelings; disconnected from discomfort.

| VICTIM | Self-denial of personal power; self-victimization or allowing others to victimize; persecution by others.

| HOLDING TOGETHER | Energy held in, holding it together under pressure. Contracted energy field.

| ARROGANCE | Spiritual arrogance, political arrogance, misuse of power, manipulation and control.

The Mask represents an unconscious or conscious need to protect, avoid, or survive. It was developed as tool to live through what was happening in early childhood. It creates a reality that is fabricated as a defense in order to avoid further wounding.

In our present day culture we are facing an epidemic of *soul murder* as psychologist Alice Miller has termed it. The Mask represents the shell or outer layer of energy of how we have creatively defended ourselves in order to survive or "go on being". When a Mask becomes comfortable, we have gone into the next phase of relationship with it – we believe the Mask is us. It has become part of our identity. It is a skin we wear and present to the outer world. We have embraced and merged with our *False Self*. (The *False Self* is the illusionary part of our make-up that represents who we are not. It becomes our split off self or *Shadow Self*).

EXAMPLES OF MASK ACTIVATION AND SELF-IDENTIFICATION AT DIFFERENT STAGES OF DEVELOPMENT

| CHILDHOOD MASKS | Develop in order to escape hurts, humiliations, shame, blame, terror. The Mask created by the infant, or child is to survive the experience.

The Mask separates us from the true child that is open, wonder-filled, vulnerable, flowing and free. The Mask will protect the child in order to withdraw into other realms or become secretive. The child will escape into the Mask identity and can eventually believe this is its identity.

Masks in childhood also develop in response to adult Masks. Children see through the untruth being played out around them such as lies, deceit, betrayal and abandonment to name but a few inauthentic adult behaviors.

The child-like part of us reacts in order to survive. It can get pissed-off, or become a warrior or victim. How we react with a Mask countering the energy overpowering us is unique to each individual. The pattern begins at birth and travels with us until we make a choice to transform.

| ADULT MASKS | Develop in stages to comply with dominant cultural myths, societal "norms" or rules, or family roles that are assigned and adopted.

The *False Self* takes over to avoid, deny, defy and protect. These Masks become mechanisms for coping in the outer world. Over time they become part of our identity. Masks of control, niceness, sameness, or intellectual superiority, as examples, harden over time. These Masks deny our *True Self*.

| SPIRITUAL MASKS | When we believe our self to be our Mask, there is a profound loss (presenting as either soul loss or as ego possession). This is a profound tear from our spiritual birthright. We believe our self to be the split, "above it all". We become the shell or the illusionary self that has lost a connection with God, Creator, The Source (use your term of reference for spiritual connection). When we forget ourselves, we forget our true essential nature that is part of the whole of all life and all creation. (We carry the spark of the Divine within us).

Masks of Arrogance and Superiority, the "power-over others" model becomes justified, rigidified and acted out.

| THE SHADOW | The Shadow side of us (and we all have this as part of our human experience) is activated over time either consciously, or unconsciously. We have a choice at every moment to act out negatively, or to shift it.

My definition of evil is this..."The conscious intention to do harm to another person, being, place or thing." This is the aspect of a twisted powerful Shadow that creates and enables evil to flourish. In order to address this aspect we must look inwardly and clean house.

The Shadow is a powerful part of human existence that has been continually denied. Conversely, some systems keep us locked in duality with beliefs such as "the light is better than the dark". Deny your baser instincts such as anger. Deny grief, jealousy, and fear. When we do not acknowledge these aspects we get into big trouble. The Shadow side will demand to be fed if it is ignored. "What you fight against becomes stronger, what you resist, persists." (Eckhart Tolle, *A New Earth*)

To acknowledge your Shadow side does not mean you have to act upon it. It can become freeing to understand this powerful aspect of your nature and to embrace the killer within through feeling it, letting the wave move through without attaching to it. We are made up of both the light and the dark. When the *False Self* gets out of balance we slip slide into very negative behaviors and outcomes. Helen Keller said, "The best way out, is through." Claim the psychic energy of negative thoughts and shift them. Thoughts have energy. Shifting our thoughts shifts our energy. When we become self-responsible and step into feeling our true nature fully, we create new alternative outcomes.

| THE WOUND | Through the process of unveiling the Mask, we arrive at the wound. There are many core wounds. The wound is an energetic memory that is carried in the cells of our bones. At a cellular level (or *soulular level*), the wound appears in the DNA as a life pattern. Also known as karmic life lessons or blueprint. The wound may be from other life times. Part of our birthright is to reconnect with our knowing – our divine state of unity consciousness. We each carry a diamond light within that is part of The Source Light.

When we incarnate, we agree in the "before times" to move from unity

Source Light consciousness into an individual consciousness. We choose to become human beings. Our inherent connection with the Source Light comes with us. We often forget this…I call it "spiritual amnesia" erroneously thinking ourselves as being separated from Source and alone. In order to incarnate on planet Earth our light body energy field slows down through the process of packing light into dense material form. We live in the material world in a state of paradox. At our core essence we remember our light body as our birthright. The material world seems to work against our remembering this by presenting us with ways to forget our Source Light.

One of the primary life tasks of humanity is to learn to heal our wounded states of separation coming into wholeness in unity consciousness. It is a big assignment and also our birthright.

Energetic encrustations, or Masks form over wounds. Wounds are experiences of separation. The wound is also a gift because it is a big clue through which the experience of healing our pain brings us back into wholeness. In so doing, we become free and our Source Light shines.

When we choose to work with a wound we choose to live courageously with an open heart. The heart, once cracked open, has only one choice – the choice to embrace and grow the soul with consciousness.

If we identify with our *wounded-ness*, we can remain victims, continually recycling old behaviors. Insanity is acting out negative behaviors expecting the outcome to be different. When we constrict energy around a wound, we create elaborate mechanisms that justify staying separate – Masks. We always have the ability to choose to shift. When we choose a different pathway, we open our capacity to move forward, and to evolve the soul. We can create a different route from the well-worn wagon ruts in the old road that have become comfortable. At a deep level we know the old patterns are not working anymore.

We evolve by choosing to create a different reality. We have the gift of choosing alternative routes by exercising our volition to move forward. In doing so, we create a new reality not only for ourselves but for collective consciousness as well.

Healing the soul wound means to have the feelings, shapes and memories of the wound but not to attach to it. The wound, when fully experienced, becomes clear, clean and full of understanding and insight. The wound attached to the past believes its pain to be overwhelmingly, the only truth. Breaking free from *wound-ology* creates inner space. The Mask no longer needs to protect the wound. Instead the wound that the Mask has covered over can be unwound and released. This creates space in which the soul grows stronger and more empowered. The illusion of the *False Self* dissipates and dissolves.

Skillful means to uncover the Mask follows with the identification and then the realization of how to shift through the wound underneath the Mask, using the Witness, Inquirer, Experience model to bring self-awareness, choice and ultimately freedom.

FIVE CORE STORIES

THAT DEVELOP INTO MASKS

Introduction to the Five Core Stories

There are Five Core stories that can develop into Masks if the reaction to perceived threat or overwhelm continues as a habitual behavior. The Core Stories develop in stages from infancy (womb, *pre-verbal* early verbal age 0-1); infancy-childhood ages 1-2; childhood ages 2-4; childhood ages 4-6; latency ages 6-8. Masks are in place by age 7 which get refined and developed as the individual begins to identify the self as Mask.

There are elements of the Five Core Story Masks within each of us. A *story* becomes a way we relate to our self and define our history. If we become stuck in a *story*, it becomes a Mask because we identify with it keeping the energetic cycle alive by feeding it. There may be an inner demand to stay in the story in order to stay safe. Our creative ability to be self-aware and respond (vs. react) forms the basis of choice to shift our behavior. We heal our reactivity to a Mask by becoming self-aware and by utilizing "skillful means" to observe and respond not from the Mask but from a witness state. *See Witness, Inquirer, Experience Model for skillful means of working with the Masks.*

Our Masks are just as much a part of us as are the higher vibration aspects of self. All aspects of our humanity are ultimately spiritual from the life lessons we learn through wounding to our greatest potentiality. We have choices as to how to respond to life experiences. The Mask represents the outer layer. Masks are keys or opportunities for soul growth.

| 1 CORE STORY |

Annihilation (Pre-verbal, ages 0-1)

Known as the schizoid wound or the annihilation trauma, the split that develops from traumatic overwhelm is the… "I'm out of here" split from the physical world. The defense reaction is to *leave the experience because it is too much* to endure. It is a primordial reaction related to protection in *pre-verbal* stages of infancy. If the reaction becomes habitual it can develop into a Mask. Habituation happens when an experience happens over and over again. The feeling tone is the same, trauma, overwhelm, life threatening.

The Mask that develops can also be experienced as being "above it all". Another way to view this is the Mask of escapism or fantasy. The Mask helps the person survive or feel in control by going into another world or by looking down on what is happening. Splitting protects the infant from feeling the overwhelming experience. This Mask can also contribute to *spiritual escapism*. Spiritual escapism represents skipping over interpersonal work, becoming un-grounded in life or being unable to make decisions. The *trance state* that is induced when this Mask becomes habitual is a fog like feeling; skimming over the surface of things. Sometimes repetitive phrases are used by the individual to sooth and comfort self while in the trance. (*Trance-states* are a form of self soothing through hypnotic-like suggestions but, the self soothing does not bring clarity to an experience. Trances deepen the disconnection with repetitive thoughts that cycle around and around leading nowhere.)

The individual in the annihilation wound Mask may prefer to skip over deep, personal work by ignoring or discounting their pain. They may skip the personal process and jump into the trans-personal world of spirituality, spending a majority of their time in this self-induced feel good energy rather than being grounded. The entrenched denial of the Mask or belief is that feeling the pain relates directly to death or annihilation. The infant, when faced with life or death, in an experience of trauma will opt for "going on being" through enacting an energetic disconnection. It is a hard-wired reaction or impulse directly related to survival. The "Catch 22" syndrome arises as this Mask becomes a way of life and self-identity.

Abandonment (Infancy ages 1-2)

The Mask of abandonment is developed approximately *pre-verbal* to age 1. (Realize these stages are all relative to an individual, they may be overlapping in age and experience). The energy that activates this Mask relates to not being able to *take in* or *too much-ness* that leads to overwhelm relating to an impingement which over-powers the infant. Another way this experience contributes to abandonment happens when the infant is left for large periods of time with no contact. The message is, "you are on your own." Existing in a sea of the great unknown without reference points or human nurturance, touch, or soothing causes unrelenting terror to become hardwired in the infant. They can become inconsolable by crying relentlessly or by becoming rigid when finally picked up. Projectile vomiting often occurs after feeding.

If for example, a baby is left in a crib to cry and cry without contact, the baby enters a terrifying landscape in which he or she interprets no one is there for it. There is no contact to nurture it, no touch for reassurance. If this pattern persists, the Mask that envelops the baby is "you are on your own". Over time, the Mask that develops will be a demand for absolute contact on his or her terms, with the twist that no matter how connected you are with the person, it is not good enough. The demand becomes… "Feed me, you can't feed me." In other words, "I demand you nurture me on my terms but, no matter how you try to meet my needs it will never be enough or right." Some behavioral counselors term this the "oral defense".

The receiving and giving wiring within the individual is confused because the wave of completion in a secure relationship with mother care-giver got cut off. Spontaneity and basic trust have been abandoned.

The natural flow of being in relationship is not there. As an adult, this Mask will result in separation and isolation. No relationship will meet the person's needs. The only way the individual feels safe will be "to do it all by myself because no one else can do it for me". There is an agonizing trance that can develop in this Mask. It is the trance of moving from relationship to relationship without ever feeling self, nor feeling fulfillment because the person is always looking to the partner to fill his/her needs (these needs are projected onto the partner). The trance becomes the addiction of hope; "Abandoning the old relationship in order to build up the energy field with the hope that the next one fulfills all my needs".

The Mask of abandonment looks outside of the individual's inner sense of self to the outer world to meet their needs. The needs may be articulated through communication with a partner. The feedback is that it is ever enough or not the right way. If the inner self has not developed sufficiently, receiving is difficult. Another option of behavior for the abandonment Mask is to live a life isolated from being in a primary intimate relationship.

Invasion and Control (ages 2-4)

This is a phase of childhood in which there is an abrupt loss of being a child. No more carefree moments, no more exploring *me* and who I am. No more trying out personal independence. The individuation process gets cut off at about age 2+. At age two we are exploring our world, with sensory development as well as personality development with words – expressions through language and meaning. The child is exploring autonomy, walking around by herself, touching things, getting a handle on objects, space, family, sights, and sounds. This is an enormous time for sensory sensitivity and brain development expansion. A reflective parent holds the young one in her lap. He then climbs down off her lap and begins to explore the environment. He explores by listening, smelling, licking, touching with fine little antennae fingers. If mother looks after the baby, and the baby goes away from mother, this is an exploration into first independence. The baby may run into the other room and peek back at Mom to see if she is tracking him. She represents a reflective mirror of continuity and constancy that the baby needs in order to grow bold and more independent.

If the autonomy of the child is stopped by trauma the child does not have a reflective parent with whom to connect. The individuation process gets cut-off. The child is immediately expected to act as someone older than his or her years. The child may be expected either verbally or non-verbally to grow up over night. Roles are assigned that may be confusing such as "be my little man", or Mommy needs you to be a "little mother". This equates to an abrupt loss of childhood. Sometimes, the child is expected to become the mother to the Mother or the Father. In that type of role reversal the child becomes the agent in place of the parent. The parent has abdicated for

whatever reason or circumstance leaving a child in charge of being the adult.

The Mask that can develop during this confusion is the child is over responsible replacing the parent.

Another twist on this developmental phase occurs when the parent keeps the child in an emotional infantile phase – not allowing the child to grow naturally. This is a time when the child takes steps towards independence and individuation. The parent's message is "You are my little baby, don't grow up." Other messages are: "Be seen and not heard"; "Be Daddy's little girl forever."; "Be Mommy's little boy forever." Also present during this time period of development is the act of eating, developing likes and dislikes. If a child is force-fed the child will express frustration through exercising his/her will. A healthy expression of anger towards a parent allows the child to develop boundaries and self-choice if the parent is attentive. Force or anger directed at a child develops a Mask reaction against invasion and control. All of these energetic layers and messages get inculcated into the child's energy field. Another scenario is the "Helicopter Mom" who hovers incessantly over a child. The child uses its new found "will" to survive by employing it. The child Mask will withdraw, disappear, become invisible or withhold itself when experiencing excessive invasion and control. The child can withdraw into a secret inner world that cannot be touched by the invading outer forces. On the surface the child Mask may appear compliant but this is a false kind of submission to an overbearing parent. The child can also spend large amounts of time in silent brooding or later in life acting out with a major rebellion.

Brooding can become a trance-like state to self-soothe the child. In later years the Mask will develop with masochistic tendencies such as over-eating or addictive behaviors. This Mask often has difficulty with authority figures.

Betrayal (ages 4-6)

During this period the child is developing a deeper sense of self, particularly feelings of sensuality, sexuality and autonomy. The child is beginning to make independent choices and decisions. Between ages 3-4 the child is exploring his/her body and bodily functions such as elimination and the genitals. Bowel movements and independent peeing become a great success story. If the child is continually shamed or blamed for soiling themselves, or left on the pot for hours because they have been "bad" the message that develops with repeated shaming is that the child is inherently bad. Over time, humiliation, negative verbal or physical abuse messages develop into a Mask of control. The issue of being betrayed and shamed by an authority figure creates feelings of being groundless, small, alone and unsure. The betrayal causes confusion about how to act in order to gain loving attention.

There is a disconnection from personal power. The autonomy phase of development is arrested. Relationships become a power struggle. The psycho-pathic Mask identity in adulthood presents as charming on the outside but in reality is a power-struggle played out over and over in relationships. The betrayed becomes the abuser by putting down the other in order to feel powerful. This Mask can become violent, using physical abuse as a means of controlling others or by feeling potently powerful by hurting others.

Rigidity and Numbness (ages 6-8)

This is a time period where the child is becoming more independent, developing a social circle outside of the family. The sense of self is undergoing another metamorphosis. The child is striving to navigate in the world, entering into a stream of life, making friends, going to school. The Mask that can develop during this period of latency relates to a "betrayal of the heart." The outer expression of the Mask presents as being *perfect* while internally confusion and chaos reign because the child feels un-worthy of love. Love has been withheld or given conditionally with high expectations. False love in the form of praise attached to perfectionism makes the youngster feel worthless. Negative reinforcement over time makes the child feel alone and separate from others, unloved and unlovable.

This is the betrayal of the heart. It is bewildering. It is abusive to be on the receiving end of having to get love by being perfect. Or by being compared to others. It becomes dangerous to show your emotions. If you cry, you are a sap, worthless again, discarded and dismissed. You are shamed for having emotions.

The Mask encrusted over the wounded heart of the child becomes one of numbness. There is a frozen quality to this Mask because the child becomes emotionally arrested at the age it forms. The outer smile is rigid and strained. The "good girl" or "good boy" Mask behavior disconnects the child from a sense of self. The child may experience herself as being blank with no emotional response. All response comes from the mind desperately trying to figure out what is wanted and how the perfect behavior should look.

CONCLUSION: MASK ACTIVATION

The ages presented are energetic forms of development not based upon psychology. The Masks are energetic and are formed in reaction to repeatedly abusive behaviors perpetrated upon the child whether these are conscious or unconscious.

Masks take time to develop but once a Mask is in place by age 7 or 8, it becomes part of the individual's way of coping and eventually the person's identity. Masks get activated when a pattern or behavior challenges the individual. A clue to knowing when a Mask has been activated is: everything becomes black or white, right or wrong. The ability to discern and be in contact with the experience is lost. Judgment prevails. A sense of in-authenticity arises, chaos, groundlessness, or defensiveness comes roaring to the forefront. The Mask is in *reactive* mode and is firing on all cylinders. Reactions may arise in combinations.

The Mask represents an unconscious need to avoid pain, it creates an illusionary reality which is a fabricated defense covering over deeper emotional and spiritual truths. Becoming aware that a Mask has been activated is the first step in healing it.

THE GUIDED MEDITATION ON THE MASK

| 1 | Skillful Practice for Working with Masks

When you become conscious a Mask has been activated you can choose to change your relationship with the Mask. How do you choose to commit to change? The familiarity of an old story being re-run is the awakener. Masks are activated from past history or how we are fantasizing about the future.

When we are in the present moment we are authentic and expressing the *True Self*. Reflect for a moment on how you experience yourself in your authenticity. What feeling arises inside your authentic self? Recollect times, places, experiences and spaces when you have felt yourself in your truth. Connect with your true essence. Let this experience become more solid and present inside you, taking root deep within. What do you require to be in contact with yourself?

Be aware of feeling your body felt sense in your authenticity. Nothing is being asked of you. There is no tension, no pulling, no pushing, no pressure. It is just you being yourself in spaciousness, allowing breath and your true self. Imagine living from this experience. Imagine and envision living from your true essence.

Now, connect with one of the Masks from your history, a core story and allow it to be activated. Notice also that, in the activation, there is something about the Mask that is part of your true nature. Take a moment to recognize the quality of your true nature in the Mask. Observe it.

The essential quality of your true nature connects deeply inside you. Feel or sense the energetic cords of the encrusted Mask. Witness how the cords feel. Review how that essential quality has provided strength, power

Skillful Practice
Worksheet

and survival for you over time.

Where is the distortion in the Mask? Imagine both Mask and authentic self sitting side by side. Feel where you began to give the Mask energy so that it will stay with you and keep you safe. Feel where you began to feed it through your behavior, your beliefs, your images. Experience how you identify yourself with the Mask. You built a relationship and gave the Mask life energy. You did this through creating certain behavioral patterns through your cords of attachment. There is an investment in keeping the Mask intact for survival.

Experience how you feed the Mask through the bargains you make with yourself. Hear those voices. Now bring up the voice of the Mask that is present. Choose one to work with in the following ceremony.

Skillful Practice
Worksheet

THE CEREMONY FOR HEALING THE MASK

Create a Mask. If you choose to work this practice with the Mask, you can make a face cast with plaster bandages following the directions from the craft store where you buy the bandages. You can do this in pairs taking turns casting the face Mask with one another. Once the Mask is cast create a circle of corn meal and tobacco to form an altar for yourself to sit inside, facing your Mask. Bring a journal and a pen and sit down facing the Mask, letting the Mask speak to you fully.

Activate the Mask's voice. How old is it? When was it created? How does it become activated? What emotions is the Mask expressing? What are its fears? What is its purpose for existence? What does the Mask believe itself to be? How are you attached to it? How do you identify with the Mask? What are the behavioral reactions and patterns of the Mask? What does the Mask need in order to soften, to change?

Hear the Mask. Let it speak. Invite its power, energy and its wisdom to educate you fully. Become the witness in this exercise and journal as the voice of the Mask speaks to you. Listen to it until it has run its course. Next is your opportunity to speak to the Mask. Hold nothing back. Do not edit yourself. Just let your voice speak to the Mask. Say whatever arises.

If you are committing to change your relationship with the Mask now is the time to do it in this ceremony. You can commit to accepting this part of yourself. Bring it into your heart, recognizing without shame or guilt when it becomes activated. You are accepting a part of yourself. Merging the power and energy of the Mask within you shifts the Mask from the encrustation energy field into your very "ground of being". The energy becomes part of you in the present moment. You are able to express your true life force with

Skillful Practice
Worksheet

no defense. Say whatever arises and journal it. Accept yourself.

At the end of the ceremony, erase the circle of the altar. Take your Mask out into nature and place it in a certain place that you will visit each day to talk to it. Learn more about your defense and when it gets activated. Understand and give space for other choices you can make in your life. Get to know everything you need to know about the Mask and learn how to merge the power of the Mask with your *True Self*. Own your shadow. Love this part of you.

Employ the witness when the Mask arises. Stop feeding it energetically. Stop giving your life force to it. Be fully empowered and live in the present moment. When pain happens allow the pain to move through you without defense or holding. The pain will only last a moment.

Allow yourself spaciousness and freedom. It is through allowing spaciousness and freedom of your *True Self* that movement will happen. Breath provides spaciousness and freedom. Allow yourself to breathe.

Behavioral movement and shift happen when you work with an activated Mask. You find it no longer has power over you. It will have less *charge* when it gets activated next and you will become more and more conscious of your ability to work with it. The Mask moves from being your "challenge teacher" to your "ally teacher".

THE MASK WORKSHEET

| 2 | Skillful Practice for Working with Masks

If you choose not to make a physical face-cast Mask but want to work with a Mask you have identified, do the following Mask practice.

It will support you in shifting the energy.

THE VOICE OF THE MASK

Listen to the Mask. What does its' voice sound like? Does it have a name? Allow its' voice to speak and journal the main points.

| BODY SENSE | What does the Mask feel like? Where does it sit in your body awareness? What places on or in your body can you energetically sense the Mask, for example in the chest, the belly, the back of the neck? Is it on the surface or deeply held inside, in an organ or a chakra?

How old is the Mask? When was it created?

Why was the Mask created?

How does the Mask become activated?

What emotions does the Mask bring forth in you?

What are the fears underneath the Mask?

What is the purpose of the Mask's existence? What is the pain underneath the Mask? Describe the Mask's core.

What trances does the Mask induce? What do these trances feel like?

How are you attached or identified with the Mask? What is the Mask's story that it wants to hold onto?

How do you hold the Mask as your defense? Why is it so important to hold it and not let it shift?

How does the Mask react to threatening situations?

What does the Mask need in order to change? Allow its voice to speak and also listen to the felt sense within your body.

How do you choose to shift the Mask when it arises?

How do you choose to unwind the trance underneath the Mask?

Sit with the Mask fully activated. Simultaneously, allow your witness self to sit undefended and be purely present. Allow both states to exist without judgment or "doing". Simply presence yourself as "being" both states. Observe and be with yourself as fully human. Follow the felt sense in your body.

Journal the insights that come to you.

Skillful Practice
Worksheet

Skillful Practice Worksheet

TRACKING THE MASKS

| 3 | Skillful Practice for Working with Masks

Reflect for a moment upon a particular Mask. Set your intention to track the origin of the Mask.

Set up a mirror and a candle. Light the candle. Bring your awareness into quiet space. Breathe and sit comfortably, facing the mirror.

Gaze softly into your left eye. Breathing softly with a relaxed gaze.

| P H A S E 1 | Notice your face, the contours, color of your skin, shape of your eyes, lips, chin. Let your awareness be with your familiar face.

| P H A S E 2 | As you continue to breathe and gaze things become fluid and begin to change. You observe your face looking into your left eye. Allow the changes to register but do not get stuck on them. Shape-shifting into the faces that arise, simply notice and let the images move through you. A kaleidoscope of images may come and go. Simply witness the images.

| P H A S E 3 | Eventually, a single face will become formed and stay. This is the face you are seeking. It is the origin of your Mask. Hold it steady. Let it reveal itself to you. Allow the energy to flow into conscious awareness. Gather the information as you would gather insights. Allow the *ah-ha*.

| P H A S E 4 | Gradually the image of the face will disappear or it may suddenly *poof*. What remains becomes clear. Your energy field merges with your Mask and you become one with your true essence. Spirit, light and energy become one. There is no separation.

Finish the practice by taking a few deep breathes with your eyes closed. Allow your senses to fully integrate with your body, emotions, mind and spirit.

|NOTE| Please be aware in the third phase of the practice, not to become attached to the identity of the Mask. Let Spirit move through and around you during this revelation time.

Do not lock yourself into the third stage. During the fourth part of the practice be aware that the merging is like a dissolving into clear light.

Skillful Practice
Worksheet

THE WITNESS, INQUIRER, EXPERIENCE MODEL
FOR TRANSFORMING MASKS

When we find ourselves re-enacting behaviors such as defensive positions
or Masks we have a choice to *wake-up* in the experience and transform our
behavior. The choice to transform behavior grows our soul. This affects
those with whom we share the experience. On a collective level there is an
evolution of consciousness. Each of us has individual life lessons we have
agreed to experience and explore in our Earth Walk. The individual life
lessons also relate to a matrix that is connected to global planetary lessons.
If you choose a path that involves transformation, there is a commitment
built into your soul's blueprint to awaken individually and move forward
relating globally to all sentient beings upon the planet. If your soul's journey
is to continue to replay certain life lessons over and over again – that is the
blueprint you have come here to learn.

I suspect that if you have chosen transformation, you are reading this
book and working with the Medicine Wheel exercises.

Most of the time we are in the *Experience* part of our personality. This
is the emotional reactive aspect of our behavior. It is familiar territory. It
is always from the past (either this life or past lives). You can identify the
experience by feeling how familiar it is. You can actually predict the outcome of a situation by staying inside the old shell of the experience. The
Mask/defensive pattern is only a surface behavior. Underneath the Mask,
lies a more subtle form of behavior. It is a belief, or a series of them along
with images that form a *trance-state*. A *trance-state* is softer than a Mask.
It feels foggy, unclear or hypnotic. Trances keep us in a state of feeling like
we are stuck and do not want to move out of them. Energetically they are

Skillful Practice
Worksheet

sticky, holding us in a cocoon that stops soul growth. When we consciously experience this feeling of helplessness it is a moment that brings an opportunity to shift. When we wake up inside the cocoon we become empowered to unfreeze old patterns. The key word here is *empowerment*. It is an energy that always exists internally connected to our soul's essence. If we have forgotten it, when we reconnect with it, it becomes an energetic force propelling us forward into healing the past so that we may live fully in the now.

Cultivating the Witness is necessary for *soulular* evolution. The Witness or observer has no agenda, is in neutral and practices watching from a place of detachment. The Witness is awake, aware and present. It is the aspect of our self that has the ability to step back and watch. Doing *nothing* in an active way, the Witness actively observes. When we observe space is created. It is when spaciousness is cultivated within our being that an opening occurs. It is from spaciousness that personal transformation takes root. Creating the ability to observe and be in neutral creates time for breathing, internal patience to opens up. Space allows something else to arise…wisdom, insight and discernment.

The Inquirer aspect of our being is the catalyst part of our soul used to unite the Experience with the Witness. The Inquirer wakes up inside an old pattern and simply asks, "What is here now?" Other catalyst questions that arise from the curiosity of the Inquirer aspect of our consciousness; "Where is this coming from?" "What is this about?"; "What is the deeper meaning about?". The Inquirer is the spark of consciousness that will lead you to more consciousness. It is activated from your commitment (your inner blueprint), to transform your life. The Inquirer stops the internalized recycling of an Experience. The Inquirer hooks up the Witness with the Experience creating a vessel for intuition to move through. When the Inquirer becomes engaged truth arises.

Skillful means of practicing this spiritual model for transformation creates new boundaries, brings forth truth, creates trust in self and others, teaches you to recognize your true needs, supports you in letting go of Masks and *trance-states*.

Naming the truth in any moment will bring you into complete presence. You are observing the truth. You are no longer grasping. You are witnessing and discerning your present state (versus judging). It is from the place of discerning that you can respond (versus react). Responding arises from internal spiritual space. Response arises from clarity, insight and understanding.

W.I.E. SKILLFUL MEANS PRACTICE

| 1 | WAKING UP – Noticing feelings of discomfort, confusion, or feeling reactive to a situation. Breathe and take this opportunity to employ the WIE model.

| 2 | TAKE SPACE – Give yourself a break by mentally stepping back from the situation. Visualize yourself taking 3 steps away from the energy. Breathe. Call your Witness forward to observe the event.

| 3 | GET CURIOUS – Ask yourself, "What is here now?" or "Why is this such a powerful event for me?" and remain in neutral as insights begin to arise. Information and insights may come forth like a movie from the past. Breathe and remain detached, simply watch. If you need space from the experience unfolding ask yourself to take a moment of silence and reflection.

| 4 | TAKE SPACE AGAIN – Take internal space for yourself. You do not have to respond in the moment. You may set a boundary that allows you more time (space). You will gain insight into the old pattern that has been activated and a deeper truth will come forth for you to recognize. Once the truth is revealed, you are no longer in the dark. You have choices you can make about the situation unfolding.

| 5 | INSIGHT – A core life lesson will present itself. You will know this because it is powerful and keeps presenting itself in your life. As it surfaces you recognize that this life lesson is something with which you are committed to being present. When you find this, you will feel an *aha*

*Skillful Practice
Worksheet*

moment. The energetic *charge* of the situation will no longer effect you. You can look at it with detachment and perhaps say to yourself, "Wow, that was intense; I'm happy I chose not to go down that old path of reaction." You have transformed the life lesson for this moment.

Will this arise again? Perhaps, and the energetic charge will be less. The recognition time becomes more immediate. You are clearer and understand the activation when it comes again. As we continually clear soul life lessons, layer after layer, they become less charged each time they arise.

| 6 | RELEASING – Unhooking from the past deserves a major celebration! Freedom from an old pattern creates new space infusing the soul with energetic lightness. Take a moment to thank the person, history or experience for bringing this to your attention for healing. Again, open to space with breath and release any cords of attachment that may remain within your energy field. This is an important part of clearing from the experience. Pause to remove any attachments that have energetic cords from the past. The Great American comedian, Milton Burle said, "Laughter is a mini-vacation." Releasing is the same. It opens space for gratitude and love to enter in.

| 7 | GRATITUDE – This practice is often over looked in our daily lives. We tend to move on without honoring what has transformed our lives. When we force-march onward, there is no time for integration and the healing of what has been transformed is dropped. In other words– back to square one – no integration, no lasting change. Again, we go back to breath and create internal space with a newly added element – patience. Patience requires that we rest, relax and metabolize healing energy. Patience requires time for

Skillful Practice
Worksheet

feelings to arise and wash through without attachment. Patience is a form of gratitude. We need to create space for patience and gratitude in our society. It is a missing factor in our healing work.

Practicing gratitude. Develop 3 ways that you practice gratitude for your life. Practice it 7 times a day during your work-day, family time, commuting, cleaning toilets, washing dishes, cleaning diapers, etc. Develop an attitude of gratitude. It will change your life. 🐢

Skillful Practice
Worksheet

9

CONCLUSION
the medicine wheel prayer

To the SOUTH DIRECTION,
guardians and allies, spirit helpers
and teachers of trust, love, and innocence,
draw near and ground us so that our feet are planted firmly
upon the Great Mother, our Earth.
Teach us and show us the way
so that we may live in right relationship with one another.
And guide us each step of our earth walk
so that our decisions are made from love.
For the sake of the children, let us live in love.

To the WEST DIRECTION,
guardians and allies, spirit helpers
and teachers of emotions, introspection, the unconscious,
and other conscious realities, of thunder and lightning
draw near and walk with us in the darkness
so that we may grieve and face our shadows.
Teach us and show us the way inward
so we may face our destructiveness and
in the dark find power in our suffering
and strength in community.
Guide us each step in our discomfort
so that we do not turn away
but live the good life for all beings;
for the sake of the children.

To the NORTH DIRECTION,
guardians and allies, spirit helpers
and teachers, ancestors and ancestral knowledge,
clear our minds with the wind
that blows away confusion and chaos.
Teach us and show us the way
so that we are cleansed and learn
from our mistakes in a humble way.
Guide us each step as we learn
to forgive, reconcile, and remember our true inheritance;
for the sake of the children.

To the EAST DIRECTION,
guardians and allies, spirit helpers
and teachers, ignite our hearts
with the fire of compassion and love.
Inspire our imaginations
so that we burn away what needs letting go
and illuminate our vision.
May we live in the power of our full song
and become change-makers here, now,
for the sake of the children.

To the ABOVE DIRECTION,
Sky Father, Father Sun, Moon Mother and Star Nations,
guardians and allies, spirit helpers
and teachers, guide us with your wisdom of the eons.
Teach us and show us the way.
Let us remember where we have come from
in the Great Cosmos and our journey to this moment.
Teach us to honor and respect all life;
for the sake of the children.

To the BELOW DIRECTION,
the Devic Kingdom, Subterranean Beings of intelligences
deep within Mother Earth,
which grow the Tree of Life, guardians and allies, spirit helpers
and teachers, guide us in our soul's journey
with the lessons we are here to learn.
Help us to understand and to grow
seeds of compassion for the sake of our children.

To the CENTER DIRECTION,
the sacred human heart within each of us,
we make a vow to "walk our talk and talk our walk"
no matter what obstacles are in front of us.
We make this vow for the sake of the children
who are here with us now,
and for the unborn children yet to come.

Creator, we pray these words are heard
and that we receive your compassion,
help and understanding.
We pray that our words become our life,
and that we live the Peaceful Blessing Way.
We thank our ancestors for showing us the way home.
May we continue to remember
for the sake of those yet to come.

BY JANE ELY
(C) 2005 *FROM REMEMBERING THE ANCESTRAL SOUL, SOUL LOSS AND RECOVERY*

LAST WORDS

At this time in our planetary history it is our task to remember our true
potential and to take action through manifesting our gifts in the world.
We are responsible to heal our self and bring our creativity into the world,
to every rock, plant, cloud, child, elder, animal, winged creature, watery
world, crawling nation, swimming nation…and so on. We are inter-related
with all life and as a fragile species, perhaps the most vulnerable species
upon the Earth, and the most destructive species, it is time for us to correct
what we have destroyed. It is time for us to come back into balance. It is
our responsibility to live together with all life forms in harmony. It is our
responsibility to live peacefully and consciously. We have this sacred trust
that has been given to us from The-Great-Mystery-That-Moves-Through-
All-Things. The trust is to live upon Mother Earth to our highest and
best potential – nothing less. This is our birthright as sentient beings upon
this unique living planet in our galaxy. A universal truth is, "As one grows
and changes, so do we all." One individual living consciously adds energy
to the entire collective consciousness. Never before have we faced such a
crisis of deliberate environmental abuse, war, greed, leadership deceit and
chaos. Money is not our god. It will not bring back one species that has
vanished. Money will not bring back one medicine plant that we need in
order to heal. Money will not keep safe the power mongers of "the world
management team" hiding in their bunkers. Money will not heal children
dismembered by land bombs nor raped women. Money has energy, make
no mistake about that. Changing our attitude from greed to gratitude is the
money energy shift. That's probably another book.

Resistance to change, ignorance and complacency are the three greatest shadows we face when we look at our collective and individual reflection in the mirror. When we resist, we empower the shadow nature that wants us to stay stuck in the malignant cycle. It we continue to resist, we will perish. If we continue to stay stuck inside our comfort zones, we will devolve. We have the tools and skills to boot ourselves into the new paradigm. The new paradigm operates from a different reality than the one we inhabit now. We have the potential to live in balance and harmony. Utilizing the ancient tools of the Medicine Wheel in the present moment is a way to dissolve resistance, educate, activate and move into a positive outcome.

This book provides skills and tools for personal healing and collective consciousness awakening. Use it and your life will change. Mess around and give the practices "lip service" and your ego will have a field day. Get serious with your spiritual self. We are at Choice Point. In fact we have passed Choice Point. It is time to move forward as activists and empowered beings. Coming into Balance through activating your true potential is a way through the Gordian knot we have created. In order to unwind what we have created and activate other aspects of our creative potentials in the world we must first heal our spiritual energy bodies. If we do not align with our spiritual aspect, we will continue to re-create disaster after disaster because we are out of alignment with our *soulular-self*. We have all the creative possibilities, capacities and potential to change. Do we have the spiritual will to do so?

Aligning with your spiritual being is the starting point, here and now. "The secret to change is to focus all your energy, not on fighting the old, but on building the new." (Socrates). Becoming a spiritual change maker is being an interpreter. Interpreters bridge the language and gaps bringing conscious connections from culture to culture, from the past into the present. What is your commitment to living on Mother Earth, NOW? 🐢

WITH BLESSINGS, GREAT LOVE AND
DEEP PRAYERS FOR ALL BEINGS.

Jane

Dr. Jane Ely can be reached at www.drjaneely.net and her non-profit 501 c (3) school *The Peacemaker School of Spiritual Healing*, www.peacemakerschool.org.

ACKNOWLEDGEMENTS

With gratitude, I thank each one of my elders, teachers, and clients all of whom have made deep contributions to this book.

Grateful thanks to Traci Slatton at Parvati Press for saying yes to this book and for manifesting it with ease and grace.

Most importantly, I thank Susan Caldwell, book designer, for her vision and artistry bringing the concepts of the Medicine Wheel into tangible form. Susan's contributions creatively illustrate some of the most important and difficult text. It would be a very dull book indeed without Susan's incredible talent.

I thank Terrie Duda Harris for reading and editing. Especially for her words of wisdom… "What exactly is your point?" For Suzanne McCreight's reading and feedback, nicely telling me about my run-on sentences. I am very grateful for friends and colleagues encouragement and wisdom, Debby Lowe-Cummings, Roddey Cohn, Susan Wintrop, Carol Hart, Don Moses and Rosa Bergola.

WA-DO, WALLALIN. *Jane*

SELECTED BIBLIOGRAPHY AND
RECOMMENDED READING LIST

ACHTERBERG, Jeanne. *Imagery in Healing: Shamanism and Modern Medicine*. Boston: New Science Library, Shambhala, 1985.

ARRIEN, Angeles. *The Four Fold Way: Walking the Paths of the Warrior, Teacher, Healer and Visionary*. New York: HarperCollins, 1993.

BERRY, Thomas. *The Dream of the Earth*. San Francisco: Sierra Club Books, 1988.

BOPP, Judie; Michael Bopp; Lee Brown; Phil Lane Jr. *The Sacred Tree: Reflections on Native American Spirituality*. Lethgridge, Alberta: Four Worlds International Institute, 1984.

CLOW, Barbara Hand. *The Pleiadian Agenda: A New Cosmology for the Age of Light*. Santa Fe: Bear and Company, 1996.

ELIADE, Mircea. *Shamanism: Archaic Techniques of Ecstasy*. Translated by Willard R. Trask. Princeton, New Jersey: Princeton University Press, 1964.

ELY, Jane. *Remembering the Ancestral Soul: Soul Loss and Recovery*. Bloomington, Indiana: Author House Press, 2005.

FOX, Matthew. *A Spirituality Named Compassion*. San Francisco: Harper, 1979.

_____ *Creation Spirituality: Liberating Gifts for the People's of the Earth*. San Francisco: Harper, 1991.

HALL, Judy. *The Crystal Bible: Volumes 1, 2, 3*. London: Octopus Publishing Group, Ltd., 2009.

HOFFMAN, Chris. *The Hoop and the Tree: A Compass for Finding A Deeper Relationship With All Life*. San Francisco: Council Oak Books, 2000.

GHANDI. Copyright: *Navajivan Trust*. A non-profit production of Voltas Limited. Bombay, India: Voltas Limited, *1983*.

MELODY. *Love is in the Earth – A Kaleidoscope of Crystals/Update*. Wheat Ridge, Co: Earth-Love Publishing House, 1999.

RED STAR, Nancy. *Star Ancestors: Extraterrestrial Contact in the Native American Tradition*. Rochester, VT: Bear and Company, 2000.

REIS, Patricia. *Through the Goddess*. New York: Continuum Publishing Company, 1995.

ROBERTS, Elizabeth J. and Elias L. Amidon (eds.). *Earth Prayers From Around the World: 365 Prayers, Poems and Invocations for Honoring the Earth*. San Francisco: Harper, 1991.

RUIZ, Don Miguel. *The Four Agreements: A Toltec Wisdom Book*. San Rafael, California: Amber-Allen Publishing, 1997.

SAMS, Jamie. *Dancing the Dream: The Seven Sacred Paths of Human Transformation*. New York: HarperCollins, 1998.

SCHAEFER, Carol. *Grandmothers Counsel the World: Wise Women Elders Offer Their Vision for our Planet*. Boston: Trumpeter Books/Shambhala Publications, Inc., 2006.

SIMMONS, Robert and Naisha Ahsian. *The Book of Stones: Who They Are and What They Teach*. East Montpelier, VT: Heaven and Earth Publishing, LLC., 2005.

TOLLE, Eckhart. *A New Earth: Awakening to Your Life's Purpose*. London: Plume: Penguin Group, 2006.

———— *Stillness Speaks*. Novato, California: New World Library. Vancouver, Canada: Namaste Publishing, 2003.

VEARY, Nana. *Change We Must, My Spiritual Journey*. Honolulu, Hawaii: Institute of Zen Studies, 1989.

VILLOLDO, Alberto. *Shaman, Healer, Sage*. New York: Harmony Books, 2000.

WALL, Steve. *To Become a Human Being: The Message of Tadodaho Chief Leon Shenandoah*. Charlotesville, Virginia: Hampton Roads Publishing Company, Inc., 2001.

WALLACE, P. A. W. *The White Roots of Peace*. Ohsweken, Ontario: IROQRAFTS, Iroquois Publications, 1997.

READERS GUIDE

| 1 | From the author's perspective, what is our birthright on Earth?

| 2 | What does the author suggest we need to shift within ourselves?

| 3 | Name the 12 Teachings of The Medicine Wheel.

| 4 | How does the author describe Change?

| 5 | What is the quote by Grandfather in the Realities section of the teachings? Why is it important?

| 6 | Name the Four Cardinal Directions and their meaning in the Medicine Wheel.

| 7 | What does our Capacity characteristic teach us?

| 8 | How does the overuse of will effect us?

| 9 | Describe *soulular* memory.

| 10 | Name the teachings of the Medicine Wheel.

| 11 | Name the Attributes of the Four Cardinal Directions.

| 12 | Look at #11 in The Qualities and Teachings of The Medicine Wheel of Life section. Name an assumption or a behavioral pattern you would like to shift. Look at the story that is attached to it. Journal as you become more aware of your behavior. What insights come forward for you to recognize?

| 13 | What are the Seven Causes of Illness?

| 14 | Review the section Attributes and Lessons in Working with The Medicine Wheel. Work with the Questions as ways to move into deep self-reflection. Add your own questions pertinent to your life experience. Journal.

| 15 | Choose a specific life lesson you want to shift. Write it in your journal. Then do the 9Rs Meditation reading it out-loud. Integrate your insights.

|16| Reflect upon a significant memory in your life and the age the event occurred. Find the age, place and the direction in The Big Moon cycles. Then go to the Four Cardinal Directions and the Semi-Cardinal Directions to coordinate and orient you to the life lessons. Take time to reflect. Look at other significant moments and ages in The Big Moon cycles. Continue to go back and forth between The Medicine Wheel teachings and the phases of The Big Moon cycles.

|17| Describe how a Mask is initially created.

|18| Why is working with your Masks important?

|19| What is the author's definition of evil?

|20| Describe the meaning of the wound.

|21| How does healing the wound change us?

|22| Review the Five Core Stories. How does working with our Masks support our soul's evolution?

|23| Choose one of the Mask exercises. Work with one of your Masks. How have you shifted? Journal your insights.

|24| Describe the Witness, Inquirer, Experience model. What is its purpose?

|25| Choose an experience outcome that you would like to shift. Use the Witness, Inquirer, Experience model exercise. Have you gained insight or shifted your awareness?

|26| What is positive active manifestation? What does the author mean by "having the spiritual will to change"?

|27| How you have changed through working with the Medicine Wheel?

VISION QUEST SONG

Ancestors we are coming, hear our prayers.

Ancestors we are coming, hear our prayers.

Ancestors we are coming, hear our prayers.

Ancestors we are coming, hear our prayers.

Ancestors we are calling, hear our prayers.

Ancestors we are calling, hear our prayers.

Ancestors we are calling, hear our prayers.

Ancestors we are calling, hear our prayers.

Wa-do; Wallalin.

CPSIA information can be obtained at www.ICGtesting.com
Printed in the USA
BVOW11s2212250215

389258BV00021B/175/P

9 781942 523000